# When the Days Were Not Long Enough

## Shawnee, Pennsylvania

## 1890-1900

by Frank LeBar

Frank M. LeBar, Editor

 www.trafford.com
North America & international
toll-free: 1 888 232 4444 (USA & Canada)
fax: 812 355 4082

In the year 1896 I was twelve years old and the days were not long enough. From the time I can remember the village of Shawnee up to that year, few if any changes had taken place. No new homes built, no new families moving in. To me in those days Shawnee was a perfect place to live.

# TABLE OF CONTENTS

# LIST OF ILLUSTRATIONS

# Editor's Preface

Some ten years before his death in 1970, my father wrote down at my request some memories of his boyhood days in Shawnee, Pennsylvania, in the 1890's. These notes were originally intended solely for perusal within the family circle, but on reading them over it seemed to me they contained historical material that would possibly be of interest to a wider audience. In these pages my father remembers his growing up in the years 1890-1900 in the village of Shawnee along the banks of the Delaware River. His stories are evocative of a way of life, centered in family, church, and community, essentially unchanged since Civil War days. Memoirs of this kind constitute the very stuff of social history and as such should be preserved.

But what is perhaps more important, they are a reflection of social forces characteristic of the time the trend from farm to urban life, the coming of "city people" to the Pocono area, and the subsequent changes wrought in the lives of the "natives." For Shawnee, the 1890's were years of beginning transition; one might say they marked the end of an era. Here can be seen clearly in microcosm the antecedents of changes still at work essentially the incorporation of Monroe County and the Pocono Mountain region within the megalopolis of New York and the eastern seaboard.

My grandfather, Hiram LeBar, who figures so largely in these pages, was in the fourth generation of

LeBars, who with their families, farmed, lumbered, rafted, and kept store for almost exactly one hundred years in and around the Shawnee area. My father, like his father, loved the Delaware River its islands, rifts, eddies, quiet backwaters, misty mornings. And he loved perhaps most of all fishing and boating on the river. As a boy of six, I began in 1926 to spend my summers at a family cottage overlooking the river at Hialeah Park one mile above Shawnee. I, also, grew to love life on the river canoeing, fishing, "messing about" with boats.

It occurred to me some years ago that I represent the sixth and last generation of LeBars to have had this intimate association with the Delaware its wooded islands, its sandy banks, its bordering flatlands and fields of corn. It was this latent awareness that prompted an earlier request for my father's memoirs and my later role as editor of his pages. I have sought, as editor of these notes, to leave them as much as possible in my father's style of writing and speaking; as such they contain a pith and humor that should not be altered. I have restricted my role in the main to rearranging the material into chapters and adding transitional sentences or paragraphs to give continuity where needed. But this remains his book.

Lastly, I wish to acknowledge the considerable help of my son, Peter Michaels LeBar, and his partner, Amelia Carr, in preparing the manuscript for publication.

Copake, New York              Frank M. LeBar

Spring, 2002

Shawnee, Pennsylvania 1890-1900.
Drawn by Frank M. LeBar

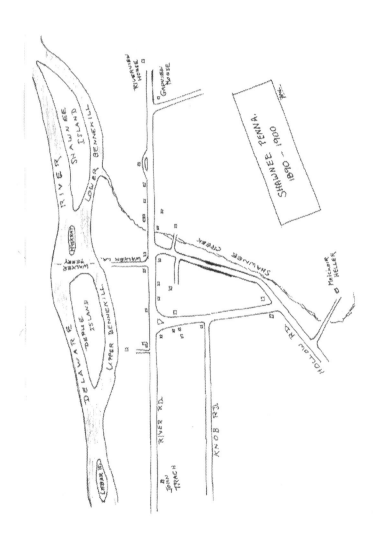

Shawnee, Pennsylvania.  Detail map showing locations in
the village.

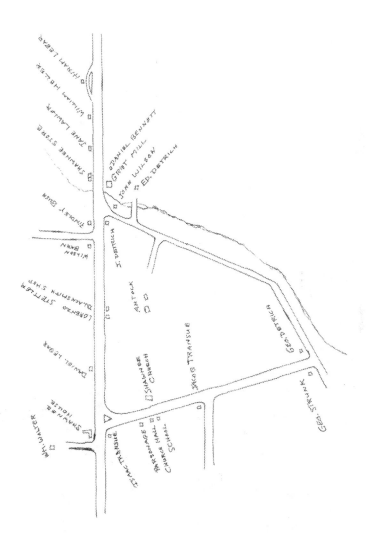

Shawnee Store, 1888. Left to right: Judge J. Depue LeBar, Sarah LeBar (his wife), Maggie Hill, her daughter Anna Hill Jeffries, Lizzie LeBar Schoonover (J.D. and Sarah's daughter).

# ONE

# THE
# VILLAGE

Iwas fortunate to have been born in the historical village of Shawnee-on-Delaware, Monroe County, Pennsylvania, located in the beautiful Delaware Valley with the Delaware River flowing peacefully by Tocks Island, LeBar Island, Depue Island, these islands forming bennekills together with the flat bottom land known for its fertility. It was this setting that must have persuaded the Indians to inhabit this land. What a wonderful time they must have had fishing, hunting and living in this beautiful valley.

My grandfather, Judge J. Depue LeBar, moved to Shawnee from Pahaquarry Township, New Jersey, about 1850. He opened a general store in Shawnee in 1859, this store [*the present Shawnee Village Store*] remaining in my family until the death of my father following the flood of 1903. My father, Hiram

LeBar, farmed about three hundred acres on Shawnee Island and adjacent land in Pennsylvania, this farm comprising the present golf course and grounds of Shawnee Inn and Country Club.

I am sure the Indians had a camp near what was called Paddy's Spring, along the Pennsylvania shore opposite Shawnee Island. Also a camp near the spring on the lower bennekill (where there is now a footbridge to the golf course on the island), and one near the spring which now supplies water to Hialeah Park settlement above Shawnee. When I was a boy Indian relics were plentiful near all three of these springs.

The first thing that I can remember clearly occurred in October, 1888, when I was four years old. The barn, just east of our house at the foot of Shawnee Hill Road (Shawnee Inn entrance), was too small to suit my father. Also the building was old and of no use. So in October my father had a "barn raising." I remember the large number of men swarming around the place and I remember the large fireplace in our downstairs kitchen and the two large iron kettles (holding forty gallons) suspended from an iron bar and a wood fire under the kettles, each kettle filled with chicken and dumplings. In later years I would hear my folks talk about the "barn raising." In those days there were no portable saw mills and no machinery to lift the lumber in place, and it was necessary to have all timbers hand hewn and ready to fit, also all pegs ready to hold the pieces in place. My father told me that during the winter of 1887 he had his men cut some of the trees on the Jersey mountain, mostly oak and hickory. He also cut the lumber for some of the beams, mostly hemlock, back of Saw Creek Club. He had Jim Treible, who lived on Dutch Hill Road [*now Mosier's Knob Road*], superintend the job. Jim was expert at getting the pieces ready so they would fit the day of the "raising." George Smith, who worked for us as hired man, hewed all the timbers by hand, using a broad ax. On the day of the raising they used long pike poles, ropes and ladders.

Our new barn was 110 feet long, 60 feet wide, with two drive-ins to unload grain and hay. The haymow held one hundred tons when full, and room to store forty acres wheat, twenty acres oats. The rye was stacked in the fields, also corn stalks. The barn was fitted with a track around the top, just beneath the roof. The hay was lifted by a large fork (each fork load weighing about three hundred lbs.). As the top of the fork hit the track the hay could be conveyed to any part of the mow, and by pulling a rope the hay dropped in place. In the 1890's we did all our threshing by horse power. Two horses were put on a treadmill, thus producing the power to run the thresher. A belt ran from the tread to the threshing machine. We usually threshed on Saturday (no school). My brother John pitched the sheaves onto the threshing machine table, brother Harry fed the sheaves into the machine, and I took care of the wheat, oats or rye as it came from the machine. We had half-bushel measures. The grain was carried by a trough to the measure. I would empty the measures as they filled, carrying them into the granary. We had fine large bins one for wheat, one for corn, one for oats, one for rye and one for buckwheat.    It was a dusty job to say the least. Later my father replaced the horse power with a gasoline engine.

The first church in Smithfield was built down near the river on what is now the Kautz farm [*north of the present DWGNRA Hialeah picnic ground*].    The remains of the foundation were visible until recently; also old coins have been found near the foundation. Then in 1752 a stone church was erected where the Shawnee Presbyterian Church now stands.    The church was remodeled in 1853, an addition being made to the front.    The original beams are still in the present church, also the original sounding board. There are many graves in the adjoining cemetery dating back to the early settlers of Shawnee.

One of the first roads in the East extended from Kingston, New York, down the Delaware Valley to the Pahaquarry Copper Mine.    This road was known as the "Old Mine Road" and was used to haul ore from the mine to Esopus, New York.    I visited this mine with several other boys in the year 1896.    At that time it was a hole in the mountain with a narrow gauge railroad track on which they brought the ore to be loaded in wagon bodies.    Three other boys were with me.    We had a lantern and rope and could enter the mine for a distance of about twenty feet, where it was blocked by fallen rock.    The mine was sold to a New York company in 1900.    They built an oxidizing smelter, a grinder, and a switch back railroad up the mountain and proceeded to mine copper.    About $1,000,000 worth of stock was sold but the investors lost their money, as the percentage of copper was too low to pay to mine it.    Later the buildings were dismantled. The only thing left is the large hole in the mountain where the rock was removed. A boys' camp now [*in 1959*] occupies the land where the smelter was originally located.

A stone mill was built in Shawnee, the first flour and grist mill in Smithfield Township. Flour was ground, loaded on boats and floated down the river to Philadelphia. Charles Turn, who [*in 1959*] lived on the Turn farm located about four miles up the river from Shawnee, told me that his grandfather brought grists to this mill on horseback, there being no river road at that time, only a trail along the river. I attended the Turn auction sale about 1910 and bought the ox yoke that had belonged to Mr. Turn's grandfather.

\* \* \* \*

In the year 1896 I was twelve years old and the days were not long enough. From the time I can remember the village of Shawnee up to that year, few if any changes had taken place. No new homes built, no new families moving in. To me in those days Shawnee was a perfect place to live. We knew everybody, and when Labor Day arrived we knew school days were at hand and I was glad when school opened. There was something about that one-room schoolhouse [*on what is now the parking lot of Shawnee Presbyterian Church*] that the boys and girls miss today.

We were one happy group, the boys on the left side of the room facing the teacher and the girls on

the right.    School opened at 9 a.m., reading of the
Bible by the teacher, repeating the Lord's Prayer, and
the lessons began: 1$^{st}$, 2$^{nd}$, 3$^{rd}$, 4$^{th}$ and 5$^{th}$ grade
reading; A and B geography; 1$^{st}$, 2$^{nd}$, and 3$^{rd}$ grade
arithmetic; 1$^{st}$, 2$^{nd}$, 3$^{rd}$ and 4$^{th}$ grade spelling; 15
minute writing period; 1$^{st}$ and 2$^{nd}$ grade history; 1$^{st}$
and 2$^{nd}$ grade geography; 1$^{st}$ and 2$^{nd}$ grade mental
arithmetic; physiology; algebra, and so on.    Each
class was seated in turn on a long recitation bench
in front of the room.    There was a ten minute recess
at 10:30, lunch from 12 to 1 p.m., recess at 2:30,
and school closed at 4 p.m.    Most pupils took an
apple to school to eat at recess.    There was a water
pail with a tin cup and each morning the teacher
would select two boys to take the pail down to Jake
Transue's spring, fill it with water, and at recess
everyone had a drink of good spring water.    The last
Friday of each month we had a spelling contest, see
who would be the last one to be spelled down.
Sometimes we had singing or recitations, a real treat.
There was always a bouquet of flowers on the
teacher's desk.    When school let out my brother John
and I had to get home to go after the cows.    We
would take turns, one every other day.    When the
cows were pastured in the lower fields on Shawnee
Island it was a good long walk.

Before we knew it chestnuts would be getting
ripe, also hickory nuts, walnuts and butternuts.
When our apples were ready we would take a wagon
load to Fred Eilenberger's cider mill at Minisink Hills
and bring home four or five barrels of sweet cider—
all we wanted to drink.    Then the ponds and river
would freeze over and we would have skating parties

at night. The upper bennekill at the end of what is now Minisink Avenue would freeze over and twenty-five or more young people, including my two brothers Harry and John and my sisters Lena and Alma, would build a fire on the bank of the river and play hockey. We built plank seats around the fire and had one grand time. When the snow came we would have sleigh riding parties on Shawnee Hill (the hill road coming into Shawnee, just above our farm house).

Come spring, the days grew longer and we had more time to enjoy ourselves. My brother John and I were always busy trapping at this time of year. Then came May 9, corn planting time, and dropping potatoes by hand and covering them with a hoe. My father planted five to six acres of potatoes since he supplied the summer boarding houses. Before we knew it summer was at hand, the hotels were filling with summer boarders, and everyone was busy.

Every August an Italian appeared with his organ grinder and monkey. He traveled by foot and stopped at all the boarding houses. He always stopped in front of our store, and would play the organ so long as anyone would put pennies in the monkey's cap. Next would come Russians with two large cinnamon bears. They always put on an exhibition in front of the store, and my father would let them camp over night in a little wooded spot up the hill, just off the road. They would take a pail of water along for the bears, also buy crackers, cheese and meat at the store.

About September first old "Doctor" Pell would stop at dinner time, have dinner with us, and then get out all his medicines.    He lived in Pike County back of Ressaca, had a sign with the name "Dr. Pell, Homemade Remedies" posted where a woods road turned off the highway.    He made all his medicines himself from herbs, roots and bark.    Had cold medicines and remedies for rheumatism, fever, chills, headache, lost appetite, and so on.    I remember he wore a heavy beard, not too clean.    He drove an odd looking carriage, never remember seeing another one like it.    My mother didn't like him as she thought he needed a bath, also haircut and shave.    My father bought rheumatism medicine, but I don't remember that it helped him any.

The young people of today have been denied the fun of gathering chestnuts in the fall of the year.    In the 1890's and up to about 1910, chestnut trees were as common as the oak is today.    Chestnut was one of the chief woods used in homes, telephone poles, fence posts and railroad ties.    We had many chestnut trees on our farm    there were trees everywhere.    The burrs would burst open along in October, in fact the first frost would start them. Well, we would get a good rain and wind storm during the night, then our parents would call us early, give us our breakfast and by daylight we would be off with our pails to gather chestnuts.    Some of the trees had large nuts, some small, some wormy. We soon learned where the large, good ones were. We each had a fifty-pound flour sack in which we stored the nuts.    These hung in the cellar to keep the contents damp and fresh.    We competed to see who would have the largest sack of nuts when the season was over.    Of all the good times we had in those days

I think hunting chestnuts was the greatest fun of all. We would boil some of the nuts, roast some on top of the stove, and eat the rest right out of the shell.

We also had many walnut trees on the farm. The good trees with the large nuts were up on the hill between our farmhouse and "Red Ann" Overfield's place, the old Gap View House at the top of Shawnee Hill [*now the site of Shawnee Square and U. S. Post Office*]. My brother John would take a wheelbarrow and a large express wagon and fill them with walnuts. When we had accumulated five or ten bushels we ran them through the corn sheller, turned by hand with a handle on the wheel. This removed the outer shell, after which we spread them in the sun to dry. In a day or two they were ready to store. We generally had about ten to twelve bushels of walnuts. Of these we sold six or seven bushels, keeping the rest for the winter. We generally had one or two bushels of butternuts and these could be stored with the outer shell intact. We had no hickorynut trees but Melchoir Heller, a cousin who lived up the Hollow Road on the property where Shawnee Lake is now located, had twelve or thirteen large shellbark hickorynut trees. When they were ready, Melchoir would let us know. John and I would go up and come home with a half-bushel or more of nuts. My father bought a blacksmith's anvil somewhere which he fastened to the top of a block of wood and it made a fine solid place to crack nuts. When my sister was ready to bake she would ask one of us to crack enough walnuts, butternuts, or hickory nuts for a cake. She also made walnut and hickory nut candy.

In those days we had no automobiles and all social activities centered around the church.   For example during the summer we would have the annual Sunday School picnic, either at Marshall's Falls, Bushkill Falls or Saylorsburg Lake.   Every family attended and there were games of all kinds, a loaded-down table of good things to eat and a good time by all.   We would have three or four strawberry and ice cream festivals during the summer.   These were held in the evening.   During the winter we had oyster suppers in the church hall.   A dish of oyster soup, crackers and spiced cabbage for twenty-five cents.   My father was known as a good cook and always made the oyster soup.   They would serve from six p.m. until everyone was full of soup and crackers. We had an organ, sang hymns, and had an excellent time.   We had spelling bees at the school house and a debating society.   Would have a spelling bee one Friday evening and a debate the next Friday.   For the spelling bee the teacher would call up about twenty people and the last one remaining won the prize.   In debating, the best team won a prize.   Then a committee served ice cream and cake.   We had some wonderfully good debaters: Frank Michaels, Clinton and Webster Eilenberger, Clara Bennett, my brother Harry, Harry Treible, Ben Bender, and many others.

Every year we had a Halloween party at our home.   This was always quite an affair, with the house decorated from top to bottom.   We would fill the corners with spruce and laurel.   Then take pumpkins, carve faces on them, put a candle inside and place them in among the spruce and laurel.   A table loaded with sweet cider, homemade doughnuts, maple sugar candy, fudge, chocolate cake, plenty of homemade ice cream, fires in the fireplaces. We would play games, sing songs, and have a grand time. We would have the young people of Shawnee and invited guests from Stroudsburg. I remember that Clinton B. Eilenberger and Frank Michaels were always special guests.

We also had sleigh riding parties and we frequently got up a party and drove somewhere for supper, square dancing and singing. A popular place in those days was Mosier's Knob, located just off Mosier's Knob Road, almost directly above Hialeah Park. The frame building was round, I would say about twenty to twenty-five feet in diameter, and about thirty-five to forty-five feet high. Had a winding stairway going up to a flat roof with a railing around it. On a clear day you could see the cliffs at Port Jervis and the Water Gap; looking west you could see Tannersville Knob and the Pocono Mountains; and the Jersey Ridge on the east. Many churches held their summer picnics at Mosier's Knob. We would drive up if there were adults. Otherwise we youngsters all walked. It was a very popular place on Sundays. The Mosiers sold homemade ice cream and often cakes and cookies. It was quite a place for the boys to take their girl friends. They had picnic tables and several times I remember they had the Water Gap Band. Whenever they had something special they charged admission.

In the fall of the year, 1900, we organized the Iroquois Society, a society for young people from sixteen to thirty years of age. We met in the Shawnee Church Hall every two weeks. Would have supper, put on by the ladies, then singing from a song book we published. Then the regular meeting after which we would have a debate, two or three each on the negative and affirmative sides, three judges to decide the winners. Also we had an annual banquet held at some good hotel. I was elected editor of the *Iroquois Chronicle*, a paper to report happenings in the community. Frank Michaels was president, Clinton Eilenberger was secretary, and my sister Alma, treasurer.

My brother John was eighteen years old and we were beginning to be conscious of the girls. I attended my first square dance that summer of 1900; it was held in the brick house on the River Road above Shawnee formerly owned by the Farringtons. This was the home where my father-in-law, Oliver Michaels, was born and raised, a lovely old home. It had a large front room where we did the dancing.

The nearest doctor was in Stroudsburg, and until 1902 we had no telephone. If anyone in our family became seriously ill, my oldest brother Harry would drive a team of fast horses to Stroudsburg, get Uncle Doc (Amzi LeBar, the druggist) or Dr. Gregory, and then drive him back again to Stroudsburg. (Amzi LeBar, who founded what is now Kresge LeBar Drug Store in Stroudsburg in 1880, was my father's brother.) I remember when one of the two men who worked for us broke his leg; there was no hospital, and he was taken care of in our home. Appendicitis was called "inflammation of the bowels" and they didn't operate. Many people died as a result. We kept patent medicines in the Shawnee store   Sloan's

Linament, Alpine Tea, Smith's Cough Drops, and the like. Dr. Pell drove around in a buggy and sold herbs and root medicines which he made himself. When babies came we called Aunt Sally Nye (my mother's sister) who lived at Minisink Hills and was a midwife, went all over the county to deliver babies. Mary Treible, who lived up along the river where Frank Kober resided, was also a midwife.

The nearest hotel or tavern was at Delaware Water Gap. Hard cider was the accepted drink for men. A number of families made blackberry wine, grape wine and elderberry wine, although we never had any at our home.

The Shawnee store was always open evenings until nine o'clock. This was the village news center and all political issues were discussed there. We always subscribed to the *Monroe Democrat* which came in the evening mail. I think about one-half the people in Shawnee took the paper. At that time there were few if any Republicans in Shawnee. My brother Harry and his friends would go over to Stroudsburg on election eve, and when they returned along about three in the morning we would always know if a Democrat had been elected because they would wake up all Shawnee. If a Republican was elected everything was quiet. We had no wars, except the Spanish American War, and no income tax. The nearest barber shop was in Stroudsburg, 25 cents to cut hair. My Uncle Phil Peters, who lived in East Stroudsburg, cut our hair and never charged.

Every family kept at least one pig and most families had two. They butchered them in the late fall for winter meat. There was a swill barrel in every pig pen. This was a hogshead ( a large heavy barrel for molasses, shipped to grocery stores   about twice the size of a sugar barrel). All the leftovers from the table and all the skim milk and buttermilk were emptied into the swill barrel. Families keeping one or two pigs were of course those with small pieces of land; farmers ordinarily kept from ten to fifteen pigs.

There were few magazines or Sunday papers in those days, and daily newspapers were saved for the privy. We never heard of toilet paper. To my recollection there were no indoor bathrooms in Shawnee; my Uncle Frank LeBar had the first one when he built Antock. In fact he had two, a great luxury. All homes had an outhouse, even the Shawnee school had two buildings in the rear, one for girls and one for boys.

Shawnee had no mayor, constable or peace officer. Smithfield Township held its elections near Buttermilk Falls, the same location as the present election house. We elected a supervisor of roads, an assessor, a tax collector, five school directors, and an overseer of the poor. I can't remember that anyone suffered from lack of food, clothing, firewood or coal; destitute cases were taken care of by the people of Shawnee. The church did its share and the minister visited all families and reported anyone in need of help. As Shawnee was not on a main highway we had few tramps and no robberies. Occasionally a tramp would stop at our home for something to eat and would ask to sleep in the barn. My father always permitted this, but if the man had matches in his pockets he had to deposit them in a cigar box outside the barn and pick them up in the morning. I can't recall any disturbances in Shawnee while I was growing up. No trouble with drunkards or the like. We didn't know what a policeman or sheriff was. There was one policeman in Stroudsburg, "Dory" Walter. His first name was Theodore but everyone called him "Dory" and that was the way he signed his name. Dory was a good friend of the family; my father always saw to it that Dory went shad fishing with him three or four evenings each year and always gave him shad.

Shawnee, Delaware Water Gap, Bushkill and similar communities had no fire departments. Stroudsburg boasted a large boiler mounted on wheels and a team of horses. They built a fire under the boiler and the pressure shot a stream of water twenty or thirty feet high. We piped spring water to our barn and a water trough, and in case of fire water was carried in pails. We had no other protection. When there was a fire the neighbors immediately gathered around and carried water. Unless a fire was discovered in the early stages there was nothing to do but let the building burn. They would try to save an adjoining building by putting up ladders and throwing pails of water over the roof and sides.

Until 1910 or so people traveled very little as I remember, and they rarely traveled just for pleasure. Shawnee people occasionally went to New York, Philadelphia or Scranton. My mother annually visited a family by the name of Mays in New York. They always spent a month during the summer at our house and during the winter my mother would visit them. In 1892 she took my brother with her to

New York and in 1894 she took me. I was ten years old. We went on the DL&W and the Mays met us in Hoboken. We stayed five or six days and they took us to shows, the stores, Central Park to see the animals, and a trip on a boat to the Statue of Liberty. My father went to Buffalo every fall to buy a carload of steers. He would sell one-half of the carload to the butchers in Stroudsburg and drive the rest home from East Stroudsburg to Shawnee.

I remember the bicycle craze from 1894 until about 1900. Everyone who had enough money bought a bicycle. My brother Harry bought one. People from New York City took regular weekend excursions; went by train from New York to Port Jervis, putting their cycles in the baggage car. Then they would ride from Port Jervis to Delaware Water Gap, put their bikes on the train there and return to New York. They had bicycle clubs, and these clubs would come down the Hollow Road to Shawnee on their way to the Water Gap. Would come through on Saturday and Sunday  ten to twenty and up to thirty in a group. We saw many tandems and quite a few came through with three on a bicycle. Saturdays they would stop at our store and buy soft drinks, candy and National Biscuit cookies. Sunday our store was always closed. My brother formed a group and they often rode to Port Jervis and back. Over the Fourth of July and Labor Day literally hundreds of riders, women as well as men, passed through Shawnee. The DL&W ran special trains to get them back to New York.

We didn't know what a concrete road or blacktop road was, even in Stroudsburg. In the summer the

roads were very dusty. Stroudsburg and East
Stroudsburg had sprinklers, a large tank on a wagon
pulled by a team of horses. Sprinkler was in the
back, eight feet wide with holes in the pipe to let the
water spray out. In the winter when the snow was
deep farmers used four horses and a large snow
plow. My father regularly plowed the roads from our
house over to the store and up around the church
and school. Where the roads had drifted shut they
simply drove through the fields. Up by the Overfield
Boarding House on top of Shawnee Hill it was
impossible to keep the road open in the winter time.
In the spring when the frost started to go out of the
ground there was trouble with mud. That was when
they used the old stone rows to fill in and make the
roads solid. The "thank-you-mams" were built of
pounded stones, making a ridge across the road to
carry off rainwater; otherwise it followed the tracks
made by wagon wheels and tore out the entire road.
Farmers were allowed to work their road tax by
supplying teams and labor. The Township allowed
$2.00 per day for a team and $1.00 per day for a
man.

The minister received an annual salary and also
got the parsonage free and his garden plowed in the
spring. My father would always give a new preacher
a dozen chickens; a chicken house went with the
parsonage and in this way the minister always had
his own eggs. Peter Eilenberger was president of the
Stroudsburg National Bank. He received $83.33 per
month or $1,000 per year, and we all thought he was
a rich man    the highest salary in Shawnee. The
school teacher received $25 per month for seven

months of regular school and three months summer school. The summer boarding houses gave the work girls their board, laundry and tips. I don't think they received over 15 or 20 dollars per month. Farmers paid their help $1.00 per day and dinner free. We had two men who boarded at our house; beside working from seven a.m. to 5:30 p.m. they did what we called the night chores, feeding the horses, putting in fresh bedding, throwing down hay and straw, feeding the pigs, and the like. We paid them $20 per month with meals, bed and laundry free.

We had no sheriff or justice of the peace or other salaried officials. The supervisor of roads was paid by the County $500 per year. A farmer was allowed to pay his road taxes by contributing a team and a man to work on the road. Actually, aside from the road and school assessments, farmers paid out little money for taxes. Monroe County had a tax collector who sat at Minisink Hills for one week each year.

J. Depue LeBar
(1814-1893)

Hiram LeBar
(1847-1903)

The Hiram LeBar homestead, 1906, Shawnee, Pennsylvania. Home of three generations of LeBars.

Frank LeBar, 1904, at the time of his graduation from East Stroudsburg State Normal School

Grace Michaels, 1906, the
year before her marriage.

Frank LeBar
(1884-1970)

Hiram LeBar barn and homestead at the foot of Shawnee
Hill. Oil painting by Bruce Horsefall, about 1912

# TWO

## FRIENDS AND NEIGHBORS

William Heller and family, the finest kind of neighbors, occupied the brick house (still standing) at the foot of Shawnee Hill, to the left of what is now the entrance to Shawnee Inn. In the 1890's Will Heller's farm joined that of my father, the two farms extending over what are now the grounds of Shawnee Inn. He was my mother's brother, a tall strong man, always doing kind things for other people. He was the one who always organized the sleigh riding parties in the winter; drove his horses and a large custom-made sleigh.  In the summer he organized straw rides; we would drive to Stroudsburg, stop and have ice cream and listen to the Stroudsburg band.  He was my father's age, but in actions he seemed much younger, always ready for a good time.

I remember on Sunday mornings we always had breakfast later than on weekdays.  Seven o'clock Sunday mornings, six o'clock weekdays.  Well, on Sunday morning we always had waffles with homemade maple syrup, sausage, coffee and so on.  I don't believe Will Heller ever missed dropping in and eating his share of waffles and sausage.  It would not have been Sunday morning breakfast without him.  In those days we had no wars or rumors of wars and Sunday breakfasts were relaxed family gatherings.  My father was full of fun and that was one time when we children could join in and tell funny things that had happened.  Will was the strongest man around the country and would often demonstrate his strength.

Next door to Will Heller was the home of Aunt Jane Lawlor [*now Mimi's Streamside Restaurant*].  To my knowledge she was not related to us but we all called her Aunt Jane.  She had very little money, made her living keeping silk worms and bees.  My brother John and I had the job of keeping her silk worms supplied with mulberry leaves.  We had three large mulberry trees.  We were not allowed to accept a cent of pay but could watch the silk worms, see the cocoons hatch out, and watch Aunt Jane spin the silk. We did accept homemade cookies.

Next to Aunt Jane was the Shawnee store and home adjoining, where grandfather and grandmother LeBar lived. Grandpa (J. Depue LeBar) ran the store and Grandma LeBar was always so glad to see her grandchildren. We always had to stop in to see her whether we wanted to or not. In the winter time John and I would stop in the store several times a week and Grandpa was always glad to see us. He would make us stand quite a while to tease us, then he would say, "Do you boys think you would like a stick of candy?" Then he would give us each a stick, put his arm around us and say, "You are two good boys, don't forget to stop in again." We actually were fond of him as he liked young people and I hope we let him know that we liked him.

The next place [now Stonybrook B & B], belonged to Uncle Findley and Aunt Findley Bush. I don't recall why we always called her Aunt Findley. They were related to us through my mother, Uncle Findley being a brother to my grandmother Heller. Uncle Findley had a cabinetmaker shop with machinery run from power produced by a water wheel. He made the water wheel himself and I remember the maze of belts to run the different saws, finishing machines, and so on. He made caskets and supplied Shawnee, Stroudsburg and surrounding country. He was always busy but would take time to answer a boy's questions. We didn't like the appearance of the coffins   he had them upstairs   and we rarely went up there to see them.

Across the road from the Shawnee Store was the Bennett grist mill, ground grists for farmers, made wheat flour, buckwheat flour, rye flour. The Bennett family lived in the house across from the store on the hill, the home now occupied by Ross Worthington. Daniel Bennett, the miller, had seven children and a fine wife. Three of the girls took first honors at the East Stroudsburg State Teachers College. His son, Frank, who passed away when he was twelve, was my closest friend when I was a boy. Dan always ground a quantity of buckwheat in the fall of the year as all farmers raised buckwheat for buckwheat cakes and chicken feed. He habitually saved the hulls and stored them in a leanto, thus keeping them dry. There was no heat in the mill and in the winter it would get very cold. Dan had a small office on the southeast corner, second floor of the mill. Kept his books, paper bags, tools and the like, in this office. He had a round stove in the center of this office with a stovepipe projecting from the stone wall in front of the mill. Well, as soon as it turned cold, he would build a fire, using buckwheat hulls for fuel. The consequence was a dense black smoke pouring out of the stovepipe. On a quiet morning you could see nothing but smoke from the buckwheat hulls.

We youngsters often went in the mill office with his son, Frank, on our way home from school. Dan always smoked a corncob pipe and I can see him to this day sitting in front of that stove smoking his pipe. The only remark he ever made was "Hello boys, don't chase the cats." I never saw him reading; he just sat and looked at the stove. There were three doors in the front of the mill, opening outward, one on each floor, the one on the first floor was used by people coming to get their grists, the second floor was for receiving grists, and the third was mostly machinery. Dan had a rope extending down from the third floor; when a customer drove up he pulled on this rope and it would ring bells on all three floors. Dan would appear at one of the three doors and pull a lever which started a small water wheel; this furnished power to pull the grists up to the second floor. On the end of the rope was a chain which the customer was expected to fasten around his bag of grists. Dan pulled the lever and up went the bag. There was a mill race carrying water to the water wheel. The race was about one thousand feet long and connected with the Shawnee Creek. There were two gates made of boards and watertight, one where the water flowed over the wheel and the other where the water entered the race from the mill pond. Dan could lower or raise these gates, thus controlling the amount of water needed to run the wheel. Never cost him a penny for power. His only cost was for kerosene to fill his lantern at night. In the fall of the year there would likely be a freshet in the creek after a heavy rain. He would open the main gate from the creek, spread a large wire apron across the race and open the lower gate, thus catching eels, suckers and other fish returning to the river for the winter.

The Wilson home was on the corner [*formerly the Sittig residence and now the Shawnee Falls Studio*]. This house was occupied by Mrs. Sarah Wilson, her sister Libby Fenner and several relatives. They were ardent church workers and kind to the sick and needy.   The small stone house adjoining their home was occupied by Bill Nye and wife.

Across the road was the old stone house owned by Jacob Detrick [later the home of Ross Fuller and now the John Moyer home].   This is one of the earliest homes in Shawnee.   My Uncle Frank LeBar owned this property when I was small; he sold it to Webster (Webb) Eilenberger, a contractor and builder.   The stone walls on the ends extended all the way to the roof and Webb removed these down to the second floor.   In demolishing the walls, he found the building had apparently been used as an Indian fort at one time; there was a double wall, with port holes that had been plastered shut, and a hollow space between the walls.   At the foot of the walls he found fifty to seventy-five flint arrowheads.   He showed them to me.   I believe Chester Phillips, his grandson, now has the arrows.

Proceeding up the River Road the next place was the blacksmith shop, a two-story building [now the Kenneth Siptroth home].   The ground floor was for shoeing horses; the second story housed equipment to mount rims on wagon wheels and the like.   The forge was connected to a large bellows which the blacksmith pumped by hand.   Willard Stetler's father was blacksmith when I was a boy.

Next was the home of Daniel LeBar, a lovely old home [now the Alex Cole residence].   Daniel LeBar died in the year 1894, when I was ten years old.   I remember him well, a dignified looking man, wore side burns and chin whiskers.   He was much interested in the Shawnee Church and left an endowment for the supply of the gospel. At his death my father was appointed administrator of the estate. The home was filled with antique furniture and a two-day auction sale was held. Reeder Posten, father of Wayne Posten, was auctioneer and this was the first sale I ever attended. Uncle Dan (he was my father's brother) had a homemade hand sled that I wanted very much, also I wanted his high silk hat. My father told me if I wanted them I would have to bid and have money in my pocket to pay for them. When the silk hat was put up I stood right in front of the auctioneer. He said: "How much am I offered for this high silk hat?" I looked up at him and said, "Five cents." I was scared to death. He said, "Sold to Frank LeBar for five cents." When the hand sled was put up I spoke out good and loud, "Fifty cents." "Gone down to Frank LeBar for fifty cents." I know he gave no one else a chance to bid. Was I a proud boy pulling that sled home with the silk hat on top of the sled!

Adjoining my Uncle Dan's home on the east was the Shawnee House, owned and operated by Isaac Transue, accommodations for seventy-five people. In those days they came from New York City for a rest in the country. I dug lamper eels, stunted small catfish and hellgrammites. I had regular customers at the Shawnee House whom I supplied with live bait. We learned to know the guests as they came to the Shawnee store for their mail, and in the evening would come down to buy ice cold soft drinks, candy and so on.

Next was Manwallamink (Old Fort Depue), the stone house by the river, now part of the Shawnee Inn property. At that time it was owned and occupied by William Walter, father of Roy Walter five boys and three girls. I was always invited to the Walter farm to drop corn. In those days we dropped the seed corn by hand, three grains to a hill, followed by a man with a hoe to cover the corn with dirt. Generally about twelve boys to drop and twelve men to cover. They customarily paid boys twenty-five cents a day and a chicken dinner. A boy always went to every corn planting to which he was invited. William Walter farmed the upper island (Manwallamink or Depue Island), and we could plant a twenty-acre field in a day.

At the top of the church hill was the parsonage and then the Shawnee Church, church hall and stone school house. The history of the church has been published elsewhere, but I do want to say that at the age of twelve years I loved the Shawnee Church. I remember how quiet and peaceful it seemed inside and outside, and always pleasant in the winter time to look out with the snow on the ground and the hills covered with snow. In the summer with the windows open there was always a cool breeze blowing and the surrounding hills were beautiful. I think the people who founded that church must have loved the hills and selected the site for its beauty and quietness.

The stone school house stood opposite the church. The building was purchased by C.C. Worthington who demolished it in 1912 and used the stone to build a wall along the road on the site of the old Shawnee House. When the interior of the school was dismantled, Robert Heller who did the work gave me several of the original school house seats.

Beyond the church, toward the Hollow Road, was a home on the right owned by Jake Transue and his two sisters, "Mandy and Sis" [*now occupied by the Ray Osfeld family*]. George Strunk lived in the house on the Hollow Road later occupied by Clyde Heller [*now the Kenneth Coss home*]. He was a man about five feet ten inches, wore chin whiskers and was all muscle. Never knew him to be sick. He was the janitor of the church as long as I lived in Shawnee kept the church clean, took care of the furnace, had charge of the cemetery, always dug all of the graves, tolled the church bell for all funerals. Funerals were always held in the church, and when the procession came in sight George would toll the bell one strike every half minute. He always had a fine garden and kept chickens and a cow.

George Strunk carried the mail when I was a boy in Shawnee. In 1903 the government abolished the old custom of carrying mail on a man's back and a Mr. Becker took over, using a horse and buggy. George used a mail bag made of heavy canvas, about four feet long, and always carried it on his back. We had two mails a day; he would leave the Shawnee Post Office (located in our store ) at nine a.m. and five p.m., returning with the mail at twelve noon and seven p.m. He was known as the fastest walker in the County. Would take the mail to the old "Tinkertown Crossing," where the road crossed the

DL&W tracks at North Water Gap.  Here there was a pole with a place to hang the mail bag.  As the mail train went by the mail car door would be open, and the man inside would kick out the bag with Shawnee mail in it.   At the same time he used a hook to recover the bag that George had hung on the pole. George Strunk was mentioned in the New York papers for getting the mail from Shawnee to North Water Gap six days a week and never missing a mail. He made this trip twice a day and I never knew him to accept a ride.  When the snow drifted the roads shut he took off across the fields.

Uncle Frank LeBar, my father's brother and general agent for the Provident Life Insurance Company of Philadelphia, in 1895 bought the Jacob Detrich property in Shawnee, comprising the stone house subsequently occupied by Ross Fuller [now John Moyer] together with all the land between the Shawnee River Road and the Hollow Road up to the Shawnee Cemetery.   In 1896 he built "Antock," a three-story home with large living room, fire place, dining room, kitchen, butler's pantry and two rooms and bath for servants' quarters.   The second floor had seven or eight bedrooms plus baths.  There was also a stable for four driving horses, a pony, servants' quarters, ice house and carriage house. The view from the porch of Antock looking down the valley to the Delaware Water Gap could not be matched; it was beyond describing.   Uncle Frank imported the first Negroes ever seen in Shawnee. One old man, "Tom," always came to our house first thing in the morning for milk, butter, eggs, vegetables, any kind of fruit we happened to have. He also did the buying at the store and ran errands. The last year that Uncle Frank came to Antock was the summer of 1901. The place was subsequently sold to E. B. Edwards, who converted it to a summer boarding house, and in 1920 the house was torn down and a new one built on the property (the Leventritt home [*now owned by Walter Wyckoff*]).

In 1910 my Uncle Frank became interested in the development of a gold mine near Carson City, Nevada. He and his partners spent well over a half-million dollars developing this mine which they were sure would prove as rich as the nearby Tonapaugh mine. Harry and John LeBar and Omar Michaels all went out to Nevada to work at the mine and be in on the action. The partners incorporated as the Kimberly Consolidated Gold Mine and issued stock, listed on the American Stock Exchange at 60 cents per share. Uncle Frank was anxious to have his relatives share in the profits which he assured us would be considerable. As I remember it Uncle Doc (Amzi LeBar) invested $2000 and I signed up for $2700, my share of my father's estate. The mine never did produce. Uncle Frank lost all his money and died shortly thereafter a broken man. I lost my $2700 but learned a valuable lesson never invest money in a venture unless you have plenty to lose.

When my family operated the Shawnee store and ran a delivery wagon once a week during the summer (1892-1900), we always stopped at "Aunt Chrissie" Strunk's place on the Mosier's Knob Road. She kept one cow and chickens. Her husband had passed away years before and her brother, Jake Halterman, lived with her. Aunt Chrissie always had a roll of butter and several dozen eggs to sell and she bought all her groceries of us. She would give her order and we would deliver it the next week. I can remember her home and the many kinds of old-fashioned flowers around the house. In addition to the chickens and cow, she kept one or two pigs; these she would butcher when the weather turned cold and this supplied them with meat during the winter.

Aunt Chrissie passed away during the winter of 1925 and a public sale was held in the spring. Her home was filled with antique furniture, old dishes, linen napkins, all manner of brass kettles, pots, pans, clocks, and so on. The day of the sale I drove my car and took my father-in-law, Oliver Michaels, with me. In those days there were no antique dealers and everything went cheap. There were so many things I wanted to buy but when the sale ended I had Aunt Chrissie's corner cupboard, her cherry dining room table, and her mantel clock. I remember my father-in-law saying, "What in the world are you going to do with all this old stuff?" But he came up next day with his wagon and hauled it home for me.

Aunt Chrissie was always a meticulous housekeeper. Finally, one spring she was unable to clean her house, just too old to do the work herself. So Edith Michaels and four neighbor women selected a day and cleaned her from attic to cellar. Even took all the dishes out of the cupboards, washed them and put them back in place. The next morning they went up to see Aunt Chrissie enjoying her clean house. They found the old lady had her dishes out of the cupboards and was washing them all over again. Said she wanted to wash her own dishes so she would know they were clean.

Sometime after 1900 Mr. Portuanda, a wealthy Italian who had made his money in the Portuanda cigar, bought several hundred acres of land up the Hollow Road three miles above Shawnee. The land he purchased comprised four or five farms but it had not been worked for years and was overgrown with brush. He bought the place to raise and breed pedigree sheep. Hired all the men he could get paid extra wages to clear the land. Then they plowed the ground and sowed special grass for sheep. He built a large barn for the sheep (converted to a chicken house some years ago by Carl Michaels of East Stroudsburg). He also built a large fifteen- or twenty-room house with bath rooms and all the latest refinements. Also built two tenant houses. He then imported a special breed of sheep and developed a thriving business. He passed away about 1920 and the buildings were closed, remaining so until the 1940's, when the houses were repaired and sold as private dwellings.

Shawnee Grist Mill, 1901, with owner D. T. Bennett and son John.  The Shawnee Store can be seen on the left

Antock, home of Franklin LeBar, Shawnee, Pennsylvania

Shawnee Presbyterian Church, built in 1853. *Secrets from Pocono Kitchens*, compiled by Women's Auxiliary, Stroudsburg Presbyterian Church, 1942, p. 151

Home of landscape artist Cullen Yates, N.A., Shawnee.
*Secrets from Pocono Kitchens*, compiled by Women's
Auxiliary, Stroudsburg Presbyterian Church, 1942, p. 181

Gap View House, John Overfield, Prop.

The Shawnee House, Isaac Transue, Prop.

The Cataract House, Henry Tucker, Prop.

Buckwood Inn, about 1912

Main Street, Shawnee

# THREE

# FARM
# AND
# HOME

My father married Elizabeth Heller, daughter of Melchoir Heller, in 1872 and in 1882 purchased the former George Bush farm from my grandfather, J. Depue LeBar. The farm included extensive river flatlands as well as fields on Shawnee Island now the site of the Shawnee Inn golf course. The Hiram LeBar homestead (at the foot of Shawnee Hill near the Shawnee Inn entrance) where I was born is still standing, serving at present as a dormitory for personnel employed by the Inn. My father razed the old barn on the property in 1888 and built a fine new barn. The foundations of the latter are still standing.

The homestead, three stories high, had twelve rooms, no bath, no water, no central heat. Outside toilet and all water carried from cistern and well. There were four fireplaces and also wood and coal stoves. The house was said to have been a tavern at one time. Stage coaches traveling from Port Jervis to New York and Philadelphia stopped here to change horses and feed passengers. The ground floor downstairs has never been changed; it contained two fireplaces, a large dining room where they fed the passengers and a large kitchen.

Our family in 1896 included my father, forty-nine years old, my mother who was two years younger, and seven children ranging in age from twenty-three to two years. Carl, the youngest of the family was born the following year, 1897. My father was very strict but a jovial, good natured man. My mother let him handle all disciplinary problems. Of course with a large family she was busy looking after children and the upkeep of the home. Both parents were religious people. My father attended the Shawnee Presbyterian Church every Sunday, was a trustee, also an elder, and looked after the money affairs of the church. He gave liberally, built the stone wall in front of the church property, looked after the cemetery, gave the land for the church hall, furnished most of the lumber and saw to the building of the hall.

I well remember the long table extending the length of our dining room. With my father and mother, eight children, and two hired men who were employed by the month and roomed and boarded with us (plus three hired men who took their meals at our house), there were always fifteen at the table in addition to company of which we had plenty. Two hired girls waited on the table. My father sat at the head, my mother at the foot. As we children grew old enough to occupy the high chair we would take our place next to my father. He would wait on the occupant of the high chair, cut his meat, and so forth. We were not allowed to talk unless we were spoken to. If we misbehaved we were sent away from the table until the meal was finished. I know this rule disturbed my mother but she never interfered. We had the minister and his wife never less than once a week and always had chicken. On Saturday we would kill six Plymouth Rock hens for Sunday dinner, and every Sunday morning we made ice cream in a six-quart freezer. My Uncle Phil Peters and family were invited as often as possible, also Aunt Bell Knapp, Aunt Sally Nye and others. My father was very strict about Sunday; we were not allowed to go swimming and cards were forbidden. Nor were we allowed to go to a baseball game on Sunday and to this day I have never gone swimming on Sunday or attended a Sunday baseball game.

I remember my mother never interfered when we were punished for doing wrong, but whenever my brother got in trouble, which was often, she would talk with him and say, "Now John, whatever you do, tell the truth and you will never regret it." We all felt free to go to her with our troubles; she never tried to shield us, but was always fair in her decisions and always counseled us to be honest and truthful. Since she had eight children and insisted that she take care of them herself my mother was seldom idle. She did all the mending for the entire family. We frequently had guests and it fell to her to help entertain them. My oldest sister, age twenty, planned all the meals, made all the desserts, pies, cookies, cake, ice cream and so on. She also saw to it that the house was in order.

May 12th was corn planting time and time to go barefoot.  The only thing we boys wore in the summer was a pair of pants and a shirt.  Come school time, September 4th or 5th, we would put on shoes and long stockings.  About November 1st we added long woolen underwear    long sleeves and legs, rather heavy material.  Mrs. Bittenbender came regularly to make shirts for the boys of yardage material from our (Shawnee) store.  We wore overalls from the store, but my father always took us to town to buy suits for Sunday and special occasions.  Mrs. Bittenbender also made all the girls' clothing.  She would be at our house several times a year and stay several weeks at a time.  At school we boys wore overalls and a shirt; I do not remember owning a tie until I entered the East Stroudsburg Normal School.  Wore a cap until I went there to school, then a derby.

From  about May 12th until October 15th we went to the river and washed with soap and water, at the same time getting in some swimming.  From October 15th until the following May we used a galvanized tub shaped like a bath tub, light in weight.  We would pour several pails of water in the tub, sit down in it, and wash.  This we did as often as we were told    ideally once a week

Until 1892 our only source of water was a large cistern; the water was collected during rains and piped into the cistern from eaves running all around the house at the edge of the roof.  In 1894 my father had a well drilled 120 feet deep and from that time we had good cold well water to drink.  Then in the year 1895 he built a spring house. My Uncle Phil Peters came with a crotched stick to hunt for a vein of water. He was known throughout the county as a water witch or dowser. He located a vein and they dug out the bank to a depth of about eighteen feet and built a spring house where we kept our milk, cream, vegetables, watermelons and the like. I think we enjoyed this spring house as much as anything we had. The water was always cold and the temperature accordingly.

We had no water in the house, no one had in those days. We carried all the water in pails. In the winter we cooked upstairs (over the ground floor summer kitchen). We used a rope to pull the pails filled with water to the second floor rear porch, emptying them into large wash tubs from which the hired girls could get the water as they needed it. We boys were also responsible for the supply of wood for the cookstove. In the winter we hauled the wood from the woodshed on a large hand sled. There was a window opposite the stove and we would hand the wood through the open window, piling it near the stove. This we had to do every day after school. During the winter my father had the men gather wood to be sawed and piled in front of the engine house, attached to the barn. When they thought they had enough to last a year they would saw the wood in sixteen- to twenty- inch lengths, split the large chunks, and haul it to the woodshed a building about twenty by twenty feet and about sixteen feet high with a flat roof.

Clothes were washed and ironed in the ground floor (basement) kitchen, where there were two large iron kettles hanging within a large open fireplace. Here we had a long wooden bench and three large wash tubs. On Sunday evening the clothes were put in two of the tubs to soak over night in soft soap. Monday morning my father would build a fire under the kettles and Kate Smith would start washing at seven o'clock. First she rubbed the clothes clean on a wash board, using hot water and soap, after which she put them in one of the kettles to boil, stirring them now and then with a wooden paddle. Next she lifted them out with the paddle, put them in tubs of clean water, rinsed them up and down to remove the soap, then into a tub of clean water with blueing. Then in a basket and on a line in the sun to dry. What a job! Tuesday she came all day to do the ironing. This was also done in the basement. There were eight children, father and mother, two hired girls and two hired men fourteen in all   to wash and iron for. I can see those piles of clothes to this day.

\* \* \* \*

My father's farm in 1896 comprised in all about three hundred acres. On Shawnee Island we had five fields, four twenty-acre fields and one of thirty acres. To get on the island we had a flat, poled across the river by two men, one on the lower side in front, one on the lower side in back. Philip Transue and George Smith worked for my father and both were experts at handling a pike pole. In the summer when the river was low enough to ford, our cows could wade across both going to pasture mornings and coming home at night. The hillside land from our farm house to the former Riverside House [*at the foot of Shawnee Hill, proceeding toward Stroudsburg*] comprised about sixty acres, two-thirds fields, one-third woodland. We raised rye and buckwheat on the hillside, also used it for pasture land. Our land north of the Shawnee Church, bordered by Mosier's Knob road on the north and the River Road on the south, comprised one hundred ten acres, one-half woodland, one-half fields, and here we raised rye and buckwheat. The remainder of the farm consisted of twenty acres of land between the house and the river (the land where Shawnee Inn is now located). My father rotated the crops, had his own lime kiln to burn lime and every winter bought a carload of fertilizer. Stored it in the shed and two barns on the island to be used in the spring and fall.

We kept nine head horses, fourteen milk cows and thirty to fifty head of young stock. Also one hundred fifty to two hundred chickens, turkeys, ducks and geese, and a pigeon house to accommodate fifty pigeons. In the spring Will Heller, my uncle who lived next door in the brick house, regularly took our young stock and his to the beech woods near Tobyhanna, a place called Droviers' Home, where they were pastured for the summer. I went along on one trip. We left Shawnee four a.m. I drove the three-seated carriage and four men drove the young stock. We reached Droviers' Home three p.m., had dinner and returned home eleven p.m. A big day but an interesting one. We also kept thirty to fifty young pigs and hogs.

Shawnee Island, where the golf course is located now, was divided into fields, each field with a fence around it. This fencing had to be strong as the milk cows, together with about sixteen to twenty steers, calves and one bull left our cow yard every morning from spring until fall. Either my brother John or I had to drive them to pasture and bring them back at night, unless the river was high and they were unable to wade across. When the river was too high we pastured them on the hill fields. All fences on the island were chestnut posts and five strands of barbed wire. Each field on the island had a place on the Jersey side where the cows could get down to the river to drink, a place twenty feet wide with fences on either side and extending out into the river. The fences enclosing the hill fields were chestnut rail fences when I was a boy. As these rotted away they were replaced by wire. Formerly, all fences were stone rows and I remember there were still stone rows with chestnut rail fences on top. When I was growing up the township was using the stone rows to make the roads passable during spring thaws. They used stone boats to haul the stones and dump them on the road, where men with heavy sledge hammers broke the stones into small pieces. In this way many of the old stone rows gradually disappeared.

My father cut his wheat with a "self dump" mowing machine. It was similar to the older machines with the exception that it would hold the cut wheat until enough accumulated for a sheaf. Two men followed the machine, tying the dumped wheat in sheaves. We boys would follow and shock the wheat, putting eight bundles in a shock with a cap on top. To make the cap we spread the straw to act as a "roof" in case of rain. In five or six days the straw dried and was then hauled to the barn. Rye and oats were cradled by hand, then raked into sheaves and shocked. Buckwheat was also cradled and shocked by hand. Later, my father bought a binder which cut and tied the grain, after which we shocked it by hand. We raised the rye and buckwheat on the hillside fields.

We had a lime kiln located on a road from the farm house down to the river, where we forded the river to Shawnee Island. The kiln was laid up with field stones and lined on the inside with clay. It had to be relined every two years or so. My father burned all his own lime up to 1895. I was eleven years old then and remember burning lime always in the winter time. First a layer of short, split chestnut wood, then on top of the wood a three-foot deep layer of chestnut coal, then broken pieces of limestone rock to fill the kiln to the top. Over the top a layer of clay. They lighted the wood at the bottom to start the coal burning, then did nothing to it for a week when there would be a kiln full of pure lime. Afterward, they shoveled it into a wagon body and hauled it to the fields where it was put in heaps and later spread over the land. In 1895 a company started burning lime for commercial use at Portland. My father and other farmers found they could buy the lime, haul it home and spread it on the fields much cheaper and easier than burning it themselves. Still later lime was put up in 100 pound bags and sold by the bag. This was the end of lime kilns. When C.C. Worthington built the golf course at Shawnee Inn our old lime kiln was demolished.

In the 1890's the average family experienced a marked change in diet come winter. None of the stores carried fresh vegetables during the winter months. Most people butchered in the fall and during the winter lived on sausage, pork, wheat and buckwheat cakes, stored potatoes, pies, puddings and home baked bread. However, our family fared somewhat better in this respect. My father bought a carload of corn-fed and fattened steers every fall, and every ten days or so throughout the winter we killed a steer and two or three hogs. We sold beef, sausage and scrapple at the store and had one man, George Smith, who made all the sausage. Thus we had beef as well as pork throughout the winter months.

In the fall we made apple butter, gathered honey, put up a barrel of sauerkraut. We canned peaches, beans, pears, plums, gages, huckleberries, elderberries, red and black raspberries, high blackberries, spiced and pickled peaches, seckel pears; we dried peaches, pears, apples, sweet corn, hops (to make yeast for bread). We had a cave under the barn which kept vegetables from freezing and they would last most of the winter. We stored potatoes, apples, cabbages, beets, carrots, turnips, parsnips. The potato cellar held two hundred bushels of potatoes. In the spring we had fresh parsnips, dandelions, horse radish and rhubarb. In the fall we pickled beets and cucumbers and put up mustard pickles.

We butchered and made sausage, scrapple, head cheese, liverwurst, tripe and souse. Also cured all our own hams and bacon. For casing in which to stuff the sausages we cleaned the intestines, scraping the outer skin, then turning them inside out and scraping again, so that they were perfectly clean. After soaking six hours in salt water they were ready to use. We also butchered beef. Had steaks, roasts, pot roasts, a kind of haggis we called raliegh (the lining of the stomach of a beef scraped clean, filled with chunks of beef and pork, then placed in a pickle of vinegar and spices and soaked for several days. Afterward, it was cooked and could be sliced off hot or cold).

We dried such things as thyme, catnip, sage, senny (senna) tea leaves, asafetida root (ground and placed in a little bag tied around the neck to ward off diseases of the throat and lungs). Sulphur and molasses was another medicine. We also gathered the bark from slippery elm trees, pounded it to a pulp and used it as a poultice.

In the fall we would have an apple butter frolic. Several of the neighbor women were always invited together with aunts and female cousins. They would cut the apples in the morning, then fill two large iron kettles with apples, mixing in cider and other ingredients. By evening the women were able to leave with several gallons of apple butter each and we would have plenty left to put away for winter. We raised hops in the garden and these we hung in the attic to dry. We used them for medicine in the winter and for yeast.

My father raised sweet potatoes, peanuts, watermelons and cantaloupes. When I was about nine years old he had the six-acre field just west of the farm house plowed. Planned to start a new orchard. When the trees arrived he asked me to help him lay out the orchard. He had a ball of twine about 300 feet long and a 100 foot tape measure. Had me hold one end while he measured and put stakes in for the trees. He arranged the trees to be set in a straight line both ways. I asked him why the trees had to be in line, why he was so particular about lining them up. He replied: "When you grow up and the trees are large, you look both ways through the line of trees and you will know why." I never forgot his remark; later, when the trees were bearing fruit and I looked through the rows of apple, pear, peach, plum and gage trees, all in line, I knew why he was so particular when he planted them.

While the trees were small, he set out black and red raspberry bushes between the rows. In two years we had bushels of berries to pick. He told my sister Aura and me that we could pick them and sell whatever the family could not use. Well, it proved to be a very profitable business. We picked the berries, hooked "Old Frog" to the buckboard, took the berries to the Delaware Water Gap  the Kittatinny Hotel, Water Gap House, Glenwood, Riverview House, and so on. We could have sold twice as many berries as we had, in fact they ordered ahead of time and we were unable to fill the orders. Mr. Broadhead, owner of the Water Gap House, said they were the finest berries he had ever bought and his guests wanted them for every meal. My father also let us sell cantaloupes and watermelons. Berries were ten cents a quart.

Our maple grove was located just beyond the apple orchard, forty or fifty large maple trees growing on hillside land. In the spring when the sap started running my father would tap the trees. As soon as we got out of school we would hike for the maple trees and carry sap down the side hill, emptying the sap into large molasses barrels   three or four barrels full. Then my father would haul two large iron kettles from our kitchen, suspend them over a wood fire, and start boiling sap. It seemed to me that the sap just evaporated in these kettles as fast as we could carry it down the hill. But in time it was all boiled down to pure syrup. When the sap had stopped running, my father would say: "Do you boys want some maple sugar?" Of course he knew what we would say so the last run of sap was always boiled until it turned to sugar. My folks had little sugar molds, shaped like a heart or a pig or a pear, and when it was all over we had maple sugar to eat, gallons of maple syrup for the family, and a gallon to give to our relatives and friends.

# FOUR

# A BOY'S
# LIFE

In the 1890's the automobile had not come into use and there were no moving pictures, television sets or airplanes, yet I well remember that we had many things to do and I was never ready to go to bed. On a summer evening after supper we would take the flat out where the river was deep, anchor it, take off our clothes (no bathing suits in those days) and have an hour of fun swimming. There were usually about six of us boys together with the two hired men who boarded at our house and George Smith who lived nearby and worked for us.

My father was operating the Shawnee store at that time, and after coming home and getting dressed I loved to go over to the store and wait on the "city boarders" as we called them, serving them ice cold soft drinks, candy, National Biscuit cookies, and so on. It was a meeting place since all mail came to the store, one delivery at noon and one at 7:30 p.m. They would get their mail, chat awhile, and if they were having a dance or entertainment of any kind they would always invite us to come around. Boarding houses in the area at that time included the Shawnee House (Isaac Transue), Riverside House (Moses Ace), Gap View House (George Overfield) and Cataract House (Henry Tucker).

During the winter my brother John and I trapped. We had about twenty-five traps, caught skunks, opossums, raccoons, muskrats and mink. I didn't mind helping with the traps, but I always prevailed on John to skin the skunks. This worked fine until he went away to school, after which I ran the trapping business alone. I don't know how I managed to skin those skunks and muskrats. I remember my father took pity on me and helped me   it was no job at all for him.

I was ten years old the fall I first started trapping alone. I decided to concentrate on muskrats and mink, and later on skunks, since the river had not yet frozen over. I put out a line of traps, as I remember about thirty, along both sides of the river for a distance of one-half to three-quarters of a mile. As I was rowing along the shore (on the Shawnee Island side) I noticed the muddy bank full of tracks. I thought they looked large for mink, muskrat or raccoon so I used a No. 1 spring trap, putting the tongue of the trap one-half inch under water and tying the chain to a large root. I fastened a piece of apple on a long stick so that the apple was about eighteen inches above the trap. I used this bait for many of my traps. As school opened at nine o'clock, I would get up well ahead of time, leave the house at seven, go down to the boat landing, get my boat and row up the Pennsylvania side first.

As I remember this particular morning, I had several muskrats, no mink. Then I crossed the river, near the head of Shawnee Island, and floated down to Muskrat Cove   called that because the water was still and deep, with large trees along the bank providing many roots, and an ideal place for muskrat and mink. As I glided into the cove I saw a large animal near the shore. As I drew nearer I discovered it was in my trap, and a raccoon. Well, I couldn't believe my eyes. I knew I had the grandfather of all raccoons. And he was in a fighting mood. I grabbed the pike pole and proceeded to hit him over the head. When I thought he was dead I unfastened the trap, lifted him in the boat   and if he weighed a pound he weighed twenty-five. I was so excited I forgot all my other traps and pulled for home.

Well, all at once Mr. Coon got up on his feet; I jumped on the seat, grabbed the pike pole and that coon was really mad. I started hitting him over the head and finally managed to kill him. When I got home I found my father shoveling sawdust out in the ice house, getting it ready for ice harvesting later on. Well, when he looked Mr. Coon over, I knew I must have a prize because he said he would make a special drying board and do the skinning himself. This was the first time he had offered to help with any of my catches. I took the skin over to a Mr. Stone who had a blacksmith shop at Marshall's Creek. He bought all kinds of skins, shipped them to New York and always paid a fair price. When Mr. Stone examined the skin he said it was the largest one he had ever bought and he was going to give me $1.25, a lot of money then. The prices we received for skins were as follows: muskrat, 15 to 20 cents; skunk, No. 1 black, $1.00; skunk, three-quarter stripe, 75 cents; skunk, one-half stripe, 50 cents; mink, $1.00 to $1.50; opossum, 25 cents; raccoon, 50 cents.

How did we know which holes had skunks, muskrat, mink, and so on? Well, muskrat holes are near the water's edge; they have a series of holes with outlets at different levels, arranged so they won't get caught when the river rises. The main holes always go up near the top of the bank. Mink holes are along a stream, but always near the surface, as a mink does not like wet holes. Also, we could tell by the tracks, especially a mink track. In the fall, around November first to December first, we would get a tracking snow, say one to two inches. This snow would lay on the ground over night, and early in the morning John and I would make a circle, going down along the river. We kept about three hundred feet apart, looking at every hole to see whether skunks had gone in or out. This way we could mark a hole for future trapping. We would go down to the end of our woods, near Ace's Riverside House, then up by "Red Ann" Overfield's Gap View House at the top of Shawnee Hill, along the hillside (the former Cullen Yates property), then on until we were opposite the Mosier's Knob road, then up as far as the Snyder place. I would say we covered four or five miles. By then it would be school time and we would finish our trip at the school house.

My uncle, Philip Peters, moved to East Stroudsburg in the spring of 1893. Aunt Bertha Peters was my mother's sister. They were quite fond of me and I spent many hours with them. I was nine years old when they moved. Uncle Phil gave me several Indian arrows and some pieces of pottery and he often talked about the Indians who lived in and around Shawnee and about the implements they used. He said, "Frank, I'm going to give you these arrows and I want you to hunt for Indian relics. When you grow up you will be proud of your collection." At that time no one around Shawnee hunted Indian relics and that was the first I knew about collecting arrows. Well, he told me just how to look for them and when to hunt them. I started walking his field after it was plowed, harrowed and rolled. A hard rain had washed the dirt off the arrows and I found three or four. Well, I got the collecting fever, and when they came to visit us about three weeks later I had a nice collection to show him. From then on every time they drove to Shawnee to spend Sunday, Uncle Phil would look at my collection and say, "Fine, keep it up".

Whenever I disappeared from home for several hours, my parents knew what I was doing. I found a perfect tomahawk on the point of our island and was mighty proud of it. From then on I hunted Indian relics every chance I got, in fact I neglected my work at times.  I remember we had what my father called a "scratcher"  about eight feet wide with sharp teeth used to scratch the ground and kill the weeds.  In those days they rolled a field with a heavy roller after planting oats, corn or buckwheat  then the rain would wash the relics so that I could easily see them.  I remember I was going over a ten-acre field of oats with the scratcher, pulled by one horse hooked in front; all I had to do was guide it.  I couldn't resist stopping Old Frog once in a while to hunt for arrows.  The field was on the large island and my father came over to see how I was getting along.  He said, "It looks good, Frank, but you're resting Old Frog too much; it won't hurt him if you don't rest him so often."  I didn't realize it then, but he knew why I was taking too much time.  It was a hot day and he had a quart of cold milk for me.  I was ashamed of myself after he left and I know from then on Old Frog didn't stop so often.

I cannot recall meeting anyone else hunting Indian relics until I was twelve years old, when Dan Bennett, who operated the grist mill, hired a miller by the name of George Dimmick.  George had a son, Earl, and he collected Indian relics.  He wanted to hunt relics with me, but I was rather selfish and was always busy when he came around.

I found a fine banner stone near the lime kiln located on the road running from the farmhouse down to our (Shawnee) Island ford.  The men were widening the road, which was built along the hillside, and they were digging out dirt and shoveling it in a wagon.  I was watching for anything unusual.  It was clay ground and I noticed a chunk of clay rather odd in shape. I took it and began to clean the clay off and there was the banner stone. It must have been imbedded seven or eight feet beneath the surface of the ground. I wonder how long that stone had been lying there?

One Saturday afternoon I went up to Eagle Cliff, overlooking Shawnee, to hunt crystals and found an arrow in one of the crevices of a rock. I then started looking for arrows, wandered farther in the woods and discovered what I was sure was an Indian grave. There was a head stone, a broken, irregular piece of flagstone imbedded in the ground, and a foot stone, same shape only smaller. The ground had settled four or five inches, filled with leaves and brush. I told no one except Bill Transue, a boy my age — in fact I sat with him in school (school seats were built to hold two). Well, I told Bill about it and made him promise to tell no one.

Some months later Bill and I decided to dig Mr. Indian up. We left on a Saturday afternoon about four o'clock, had a pick and shovel, got up there about five o'clock. The sun had gone down back of the hill and it was getting dusk. We cleaned off the leaves and brush and started to pick and shovel. About that time we heard a strange noise, sounded like some one groaning. We stopped and listened, said nothing, started to work again. The same sound again, only louder. Bill says, "What is that noise, do you hear it?" I said, "I sure do." Well, we started to dig again and the noise came again, louder than ever. We looked at each other; Bill grabbed the pick, I took the shovel and we never looked back nor did we ever tell anyone about it. About four years later I went alone to dig up that grave. Well, I hunted and hunted, couldn't find the grave or any trace of it. I think Bill told someone that we were going up and they followed us, scared us out, and dug up the grave.

In the spring of 1895, I was ten years old, my brother John was twelve, and Donald Campbell, the preacher's son, was eleven. The Church decided to build a wagon shed in the rear of the present parish house   this shed was torn down about 1930. When they finished the building there was some scrap lumber at the site. We boys wanted a shack or a place where we could hold meetings, and since my father had furnished the lumber to build the shed, we asked him if we could have some to build a shack. He said, "Take whatever you want but don't waste it." We found a ladder that had been left at the shed and since we had been climbing in the big oak tree in front of the Shawnee Church this gave us the idea to build a tree house. The limbs came out just right and made an ideal place. Shack had a floor, four sides and a roof. We had a grand time, would pack a lunch and have supper in our shack, hold secret meetings, and so on. Well, came fall and two of the elders notified the minister, Rev. Campbell, that our creation would have to come down.   As Donald Campbell was the preacher's son and one of the three builders, we had to dismantle it and hold our meetings elsewhere. We had the fun of building it and occupying it one summer, so we didn't feel too badly about it. The oak tree is still standing in front of the present Shawnee Church.

My brother John and I together with four other boys our age always went out Halloween night and did plenty of mischief. For one thing, we would upset at least six to eight outhouses. We also put boards over the top of the chimney of the school house so the teacher had to get a ladder, climb up, and remove them. Took the wheels off a number of buggies. The last Halloween night we operated, we took George Detrick's buggy and pulled it up to the Church shed, a building one story high with a gable roof. We stood two long planks up against the roof, one for each set of wheels. Had a long stout rope, and one of us guided the wagon while the others pulled it up. We all went to school next morning and there was the buggy astraddle of the roof. George Detrick offered a reward for anyone who would tell him who would do such a dirty trick. He suspected my older brother Harry and his pals. Well, all the publicity scared us pretty thoroughly and we never played Halloween tricks after that.

My father kept a number of steers, fattening them to butcher at various times. We had two very large animals that had been dehorned, so that they were relatively harmless. My older brother John began riding these two steers until he got them so tame that one day he said to me: "Ben (my family nickname), we can tame these steers so we can get the ox yoke on them and drive them around like oxen." Well, we got them in the calf pen and John and I worked and worked until we got the yoke around their necks. Then we took them out in the barnyard where John fastened a rope to the yoke. He would say "Gee," whereupon I would push them to the left; then "Haw" and I would shove them to the right. When John decided he had them trained we took them out of the yard, got the stone boat. This was a flat sled made of planks, about four feet wide by ten feet long, with two runners underneath. We would hook a team of horses to it and haul loose stones off the sidehill fields, piling them in stone rows.

Well, we ran a stout rope from the ox yoke to the stone boat, John fastened the guide lines to the left steer, told me to get on the sled and he would do the guiding. We went around the barn, everything went fine. Then John said, "I'm going to take you for a ride over to the store and back, you stay on the sled and I'll guide them." We got half way to the store when those two steers decided to go back home. They swung around and away we went. John yelled to me to hold on; he was hanging unto the lines. Well, that was one fast ride. When they reached the barn they made a beeline for the barnyard. The stone boat hit a tree and I flew off. John was still hanging on but badly skinned where the steers had dragged him along the ground. He removed the yoke, opened the barnyard gate, and the steers ran in. He closed the gate, took the rope off the sled, put the ox yoke in the barn, then said: "Ben, don't you ever tell anyone about this." And it was years later before I ever told anyone about the ride on the stone boat, pulled by two steers.

One year my father planted a patch of potatoes down by the river, on a little point of land where Shawnee Creek empties into the Delaware. It was a hot summer afternoon when he told John and me to go down and hoe the potatoes. When we arrived John said, "Now Ben, we will hoe four or five hills in from the ends and then go swimming." Well, in half an hour we had the end hills hoed. We went down the bank to the river, took off our clothes, and jumped in. We were having a grand time when we heard a voice on the bank. My father stood there by our clothes with a river birch in his hand. Said "Come out, put on your clothes and finish hoeing these potatoes!" He didn't forget to use the river birch as we climbed the bank.

John was always thinking up schemes which got the two of us in trouble. One year my father hired a work girl by the name of Rose Hufford. She was older than the other girls and very bossy   sort of got the idea that she was hired to boss us youngsters. We didn't like her at all. My sister baked cookies once a week and we always had a batter pail full of ginger snaps and a pail full of sugar cookies; when John and I would get home from school we would go to the cookie pail and help ourselves. Rose noticed this and one day she hid the cookies. When we got home they were gone. John made inquiries and found that Rose was the culprit. Rose had a wooden leg, would unstrap the leg at night and lay it by her bed   where she slept in a room off the kitchen. That night, after we had gone to bed, John said, "I'm going to sneak downstairs, steal her leg and hide it." Which he did. Well, in the morning there was plenty of excitement.

Rose couldn't get out of bed, and who had stolen her leg? They finally decided it was John; my mother called John and had a talk with him, told him that Rose demanded that his father punish him good and proper. She also said to John, "Now you tell your father the truth and why you hid her leg." Well, Rose got her leg back, the cookie jars were back in their place, and so far as I know John was never punished for that episode.

My brother John and I grew up almost like twins. We had our scraps and he always wanted to be the leader, but let anything happen to me or let any boy try to take advantage of me, John always took my part. We always felt close together, right up to the day he passed away.

# FIVE
# FISHING

My father's hobby was fishing. He told my brother John and me that as soon as we could row a boat and swim he would take us with him, which he did. But he would only take one of us at a time. Those trips are outstanding in my memory as he was a good fisherman and taught us all he knew. Whenever freshets came in the river he would put an "out line" across to Muskrat Island, in front of where Shawnee Inn now stands. This set line was very strong, and to it about every eighteen inches was fastened a short line and hook. I think there must have been at least 150 hooks. Stone anchors took the line to the bottom of the river. He would put the set line out just before dark, then about eleven p.m. go out to look it over , taking John one time, me the next time. He often had a half bushel or more of eels to bring home.

In the morning he would get up at five, go over the line again, take off the eels and bring the line home to dry.  He kept the eels in a large washtub before skinning and cleaning them. He also took us with him back to Twelve Mile Pond (Pike County) to fish for bass and pickerel.  We would stay about three days and just loved those trips.  My father also fished in the winter at Mink's Pond back of Bushkill, fishing through the ice for pickerel.  We boys never went on those trips as it was too cold.

My father not only caught lots of fish, but he always fried them himself as the work girls couldn't do it to suit him.  He had a large griddle, one that reached across the wood stove.  He would fry the fish in butter and they were delicious.  In fact, my father supervised much of the cooking at home.  We always had hot cakes for breakfast   buckwheat cakes and sausage in the winter, wheat cakes in the summer.  He would rise early, build up the wood fire, put on the coffee and mix the wheat cakes.  If it was buckwheat cakes he would thin the batter so they were just right.  Then the hired girl would take over.

My father also owned a shad net   a woven twine net sixty feet long and about six feet wide, with lead weights at the bottom and large corks at the top.  The net could be folded on the back of a boat and required four men to operate it.  My father's shad fishery was about one mile above Shawnee, at the back of LeBar Island, between the island and the Jersey shore. Rights to this fishery probably stemmed from the fact that my great-great-grandfather, Daniel LeBar Jr., in about 1800 built a stone house and farmed one hundred fifty acres along the Jersey shore facing what came to be known as LeBar Island. My father, my grandfather and my great-grandfather were all born in this old house.

In the summer when the river was low my father and his hired men always went up to clean the fishery out, removing large stones and old logs so that the net wouldn't catch on the bottom. Shad start running about April 15th, lying quiet during the day and moving only after dark. They annually swim to the headwaters of the Delaware to lay their spawn; when the young hatch out they come back down the river to tidewater and disappear until the next spring, when they again come up the river as full grown shad.

Toward dusk the men would leave with the shad net, row up to the shad fishery. Two men in the boat, one to row and one to pay out the net. Another man on the shore held one end of the net. They would make a circle, coming back into shore where a fourth man would secure the other end. When the net was pulled to shore they would get all the shad that happened to be in that spot. Some evenings they would come home with a catch of twenty to thirty fish. The average shad weighed from four to eight pounds. Any under four pounds were called "pink eyes" full of small bones and poor eating. There was one Shawnee resident who was always ready and anxious to be invited to go shad fishing with any of the four shad net owners in the area. After the evening fishing was over and the shad divided, there would be ten to twelve

pink eyes left.  Someone would remark about the pink
eyes; Henry would speak up and say, "I'll be glad to
take them home to feed to the cats."  Everybody knew
that the cats wouldn't get them.    He had an old
hogshead from the Shawnee store    one that had held
mackerel packed in salt brine.  Took the shad home,
cleaned them, and put them in brine in the hogshead.
He about lived on shad, mush and milk.    It was a
standing joke in Shawnee about Henry and the "pink
eyes."

One evening my father invited my brother John,
twelve years old, Andrew Smith, also twelve, and
myself, ten years old, to go shad fishing with him.  We
were seldom allowed on these excursions and felt
honored.    The men, in addition to my father, were
George Smith, Phil Transue, Jake Transue, and Will
Walters.  We used three boats as the net was heavy
and took up most of one boat.  As I think about it now
I wonder that those men could work all day from seven
a.m. to five p.m., then row a boat one mile up stream
and work at shad fishing for another two hours.  They
must have been in perfect health.

We left about seven p.m. and arrived at the shad
fishery about eight    just in time for the shad to start
running.  We had made one haul with the net when
the sky darkened noticeably and it started to thunder
and lightning.  Well, we knew we were in for a soaking
rain and it was a cold night.  We tumbled into the
boats and pulled for Jersey and the old stone house
vacant for three years and set back from the road at
least seventy-five feet.  Weeds, briars and sumac had

grown up as high as a man's head. It had grown so dark that we could see only by the light of lanterns. There was a back porch on the house and we were hurrying to get on that porch before it started to rain. George Smith and Phil Transue were in the lead with two of the lanterns, tramping down the weeds and briars.

As they neared the house they suddenly yelled "Boa constrictor on the porch!" (Two months earlier a boa constrictor had escaped from a circus showing in Newton, New Jersey.) Well there was no joke about it. I think the men were all scared. I was so frightened I grabbed my dad and he lifted me up in his arms. George Smith found a heavy stick, told Phil Transue to hold the lantern. He raised the stick to strike and when the light shone on the porch we saw only a black, crooked tree limb. The rain came down in sheets, lasted for one-half hour. When it was all over my father said, "Now boys, we don't say a thing in Shawnee about what happened here tonight, they wouldn't understand." We boys vowed that we would tell no one, but we often mentioned it when we were together and thought it was a good story but mum was the word.

My memories of boyhood days in Shawnee often turn to Jake Transue, a quiet man, always neat and clean. He was unmarried, spent part of his time working for my father, the balance fishing, and loafing at the Shawnee store. He was polite, but never spoke unless he was spoken to. When my father needed extra help at haying time, harvesting, corn cutting, lumbering in winter and rafting in spring, he would send for Jake. He was a slow but steady worker, willing and able to try his hand at anything. Never known to complain.

Jake Transue was a great fisherman, and known all along the river, as he never rowed a boat. He used a long pike pole, with a sharp iron on the end; always kept near shore and poled the boat up the river stern foremost. Jake always stood up in the back of the boat, and from this position he could pole it twice as fast as anyone else could row. He was an expert in this one thing; anyone on the river would know it was Jake, even at a distance.

When I was thirteen or fourteen years old, Jake asked me to go fishing with him. It was in August, bass fishing. When I asked my father he said, "Yes, you can go but promise to sit still in the boat and don't annoy Jake by talking. You can consider yourself honored as we have never known him to ask anyone to go fishing before." My folks packed a lunch and we left our boat landing at six o'clock in the morning. I sat on a board near Jake so the front end of the boat would be out of water. He started to pole and in no time we were in Trach's Eddy in front of LeBar Island. Jake poled on up to Walters' Eddy and we started to fish. We would float down the river, fishing, then Jake would pole the boat back up.

Come noon we stopped on the Jersey shore at a stream across from LeBar Island, ate lunch, drank the cold water flowing down the mountain to the river, then fished again. About four o'clock we started to float home; I knew Jake wanted me to catch a large bass because he was so attentive to my bait and told me I was a good fisherman. Well, I pleased him by getting two nice bass. Jake caught four, cleaning them on the way home. When we landed Jake cut a river birch, strung the six bass, and handed me the string of fish. I said, "Oh no, Jake, you take your fish with you." But he refused, saying he wanted me to have them all as they made a nice looking string of bass. Well, I never spent a more enjoyable day and I think Jake was pleased with me. I know I was a proud boy carrying that string of bass home to show them to my father and mother!

Years later, when I was married and living in Stroudsburg, Jake called me one spring to come to his house in Shawnee where he had a supply of suckers in a little stream behind his barn. (There is no better eating fish than a sucker caught in the early spring.) He gave me four or five suckers to take home. Later I stopped by with a pack of Dukes Mixture for his pipe, which pleased him. He was a man who never said an ill word against anyone   a fine friend to k now and like.

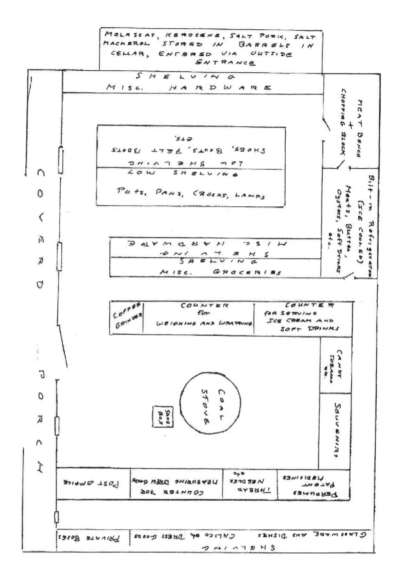

Floor plan of Shawnee Store, ca. 1895.   Originally one large room, the store was enlarged about 1893.

Daybook of the LeBar and Heller General Store and Post Office. Opening page, from 1859

# SIX

# COUNTRY STOREKEEPING

My grandfather, J .D. LeBar, owned the Shawnee Store [*the present Shawnee Village Store*] from 1859 until the year he died, in 1893. My father took over the store and post office in that year. We ran it as a family enterprise; my eldest brother Harry looked after the store, assisted by my sister Alma during haying and harvesting when H arry was needed on the farm. When I was fourteen years old I helped in the store part of the time. The present store, operated by Arthur Mosteller [*now the Della Feras*], is located in the original building, although additions and changes have been made by various owners over the years.

In 1893 the store consisted of a single large room, with a big round stove in the center. Near the stove stood a box of sand, where the men could spit their tobacco juice. Shortly after my father took over the store he built an addition on the upper side and here he put in a line of hardware, boots and shoes and fresh meats.

Everything came in barrels in those days crackers, sugar, salt, molasses, side pork in brine, kerosene in barrels. Mackerel came in hogsheads and packed in salt brine. We used a stick with a hook on the end to fish the mackerel out whenever a customer wanted any. Muslin, calico and gingham came in rolls and was measured off by the yard. The store had a front window and here Grandpa had a single broad shelf. On it were three glass jars containing candy and I remember these very clearly.

We had the post office in the southwest corner of the store and next to it a dry goods counter where we measured off calico or gingham by the yard. In those days stores stayed open until about nine p.m., as a great many people worked during the day and did their shopping at night. There were always some men who would come to the store after supper to loaf and spend the evening. Two or three of them took to sitting on the dry goods counter, handy to the stove and the box of sand. My brother Harry, who tended store and also ran the post office, would have to ask them to get off the counter every time he wanted to wait on a customer. He finally got tired of chasing them off and rigged up a scheme that worked pretty well.

Harry made a small hole through the top of the counter and had a spring with a pin attached to it which he fastened underneath the counter, just below the hole. Then he ran a stout string from the spring to his chair behind the post office. He waited for the first loafer to sit down on the counter and then pulled the string. This released the spring and the pin shot up through the hole. The fellow jumped off the counter with a yell. After finding the hole in the counter and Harry's arrangement, he made us all promise to keep quiet and he (the victim) would get the next man. After about two or three of them got stuck with the pin we had no more trouble.

One salesman, a man by the name of Bill Shandy, called at the store every ten days. He represented Austin Nichols Co., wholesale grocery and miscellaneous items, New York City. He had a fine business from our store. Boots, shoes, rubbers, men's shirts, overalls, stockings, socks, all kinds of dress goods, novelties, etc., were all ordered by catalog. We never did any kind of advertising. There were no road signs in those days, in fact little advertising of any kind. The Sears Roebuck catalog, mailed direct to customers, was the only advertising media that I remember.

During the spring, summer and fall we had a large delivery wagon and two routes: one up the River Road, crossing over at Zimmerman's Ferry (just above the former Camp Hagen), back down through Jersey to the Marshall Walker Ferry (across from Shawnee Inn) and home. Another route went over Mosier's Knob Road to Coolbaughs and back to Shawnee via the Hollow Road. We would take orders to be delivered the following week, each route one day each week. We took butter, eggs, chestnuts, hickory nuts, walnuts, lard and potatoes in trade.

I have often wondered if my father made any money operating the Shawnee store.  In those days there was no income tax, consequently he never took an inventory.  He had only two books, a day book where items were entered for bills that were not paid, and a ledger where the total amount was charged to the customer.

The day book was just a plain book with several hundred lined pages.  If a customer came in and bought something and had it charged we entered it in the day book.  Each item was entered and totaled.  Then the customer's total was posted in the ledger.  The ledger was indexed with the customer's name   for example John Smith was entered under "S" and given a page number in the ledger.  There were debit and credit columns.  When the customer made a payment on his account it was credited; if he paid the entire bill it was credited and a line drawn to show the account was paid in full.

My father had one bank account, carried in the Stroudsburg National Bank, the only bank in the Stroudsburgs in those days.  I am sure he must have carried a large cash balance as all bills were run through the store account.  For example, during the winter months men living in the "woods country" as we called it in those days (the area of Pike County around Mink's Pond, Lehman's Lake and Saw Creek) would haul ties in by wagon or sled and my father would have them unload down by our island landing.  There the ties were put in piles ready to raft down the river

in the spring. They would generally have fifteen or
twenty ties to a load   worth about five to six dollars.
My father would measure and inspect the ties, then
give the man a credit slip which he could take to the
store and exchange for merchandise. The first thing a
man would buy was his smoking or chewing tobacco,
then salt pork, salt mackerel, flour, sugar and
molasses.

As I think back, my father undoubtedly tied up a
good deal of money in this way   money which he
would not get back until about May first (some four to
six months later) when the ties were rafted down to
Easton, taken out of the river and sold to the
Pennsylvania or Lehigh Valley Railroad.  He also
bought beef cattle in Buffalo, to be shipped to East
Stroudsburg in carload lots.  Then he would kill two or
three every ten days. He sold the beef in our store and
also supplied the Indian Queen and Washington hotels
in Stroudsburg.

My father was a good provider, but he was never
careless with money.  Whenever my brother or I
needed clothes, he would take us to town to Reise's
clothing store.  A dressmaker would come to the
house, stay a week or two, and make dresses for my
sisters and my mother.  The money that my brother
and I earned trapping and selling bait to the summer
boarders we gave to my father. He kept a note in his
desk for each of us; if we gave him ten dollars he
would add it to the total, make out a new note, and
add six percent interest.  In this way when my father
passed away the attorneys for the estate paid me

around four hundred dollars    a good deal of money in those days.

My father always cautioned us never to buy anything unless we had the money to pay for it. To my knowledge he never borrowed money.  Come winter there were always six or seven families who would run an account at the store; they paid their bills promptly during the summer, but in winter the husband had no work and they were all large families.  Well, an account would get up to fifty dollars.  My brother Harry would ask Dad what he was going to do about it.  He would never say a word but make it his business to go to the store, get the general ledger, and write in the credit side "account paid in full." Some of the family found fault with him, but I can hear him say, many times, "We have full and plenty and no one is going to go hungry in Shawnee."

I could add that this generosity on my father's part paid off years later when I found myself stuck in front of the Buckwood Inn entrance with a flat tire and no spare.  Lloyd Lee was operating the Worthington garage at that time and I appealed to him for help. He took the tire off, put a patch on the tube, put the tire back on the car, and when I wanted to pay his reply was "Frank, you don't owe me a cent.  You may have forgotten, when I was a boy, lived up the Hollow Road, five brothers and sisters, father with no work during the winter.  If it hadn't been for your father we would have starved.  No, Frank, this is a real pleasure to pay off just a little of that debt." Well, I think that was a wonderful tribute to my father.

# SEVEN
## LUMBERING AND RAFTING

My grandfather began at age sixteen (i.e., about 1830) to run rafts to Philadelphia and in his later years was considered one of the expert steersmen on the river. He was a member of the crew on the pioneer trip of the steamboat "Kittatinny," running from the Delaware Water Gap to Port Jervis in the spring of 1879. When he was eighteen or twenty years old (i.e., about 1867) my father accompanied my grandfather on rafts to Easton, learning to steer and learning the channel of the river. After a successful trip they would walk home. My father always said they took short cuts whenever possible.

When I was a boy my father was carrying on an extensive lumbering business in addition to farming and storekeeping, running rafts annually to Portland and Easton. He would buy ties during the winter months; they were put in piles and rafted in the spring. During the summer he would buy a tract and then lumber it off during the winter. He lumbered in New Jersey, one mile above Shawnee, where one hundred and fifty acres of land went with an old stone house on property which belonged to my grandfather, then to my father. We had plenty of snow in those days and they would cut the logs, snake them with a team of horses to a sluice, then slide them down the mountain to near the river where they were put in piles ready to raft down to Easton in the spring of the year. My father always had four lumbermen hired during the winter; in addition the two men who boarded with us and worked by the month, drove team and helped pile the logs. These lumbermen always had their breakfast and supper at our house; their dinner was packed in baskets or pails by the work girls. My father also lumbered near and around Bushkill, piling the logs on the river bank near Peter's boat landing.

In the spring of 1896 he told my brother and me he was going to give us a ride on a log raft from Bushkill to Easton. I was twelve and my brother John fourteen. He didn't tell us the exact day but one evening after finishing supper he said, "You boys go

upstairs and get to bed.    I will call you in the
morning." It seemed to me we had only slept a short
time when he opened the door, told us what clothes to
put on    the warmest we had    and when we came
down the men were already eating. We left the house
at six o'clock in a three-seated wagon for Bushkill. I
remember it was a clear day but chilly.

We had a large wooden shoe box from the store
which they nailed to the logs in the center of the raft,
then two or three blankets and a large box with a
lunch that my mother had fixed for us.   At seven
o'clock the men untied the ropes, which were fastened
to trees, rolled them up on the raft, and my Dad called
"Ready to leave." It was a four-oar raft, two oars front
and two rear.   There was one man to each oar, the
steersman (my father) standing at the rear of the raft,
Pennsylvania side; this was the position all steersmen
occupied.  My father called "hold" (i.e., rest oars) and
we started to float with the current.  We were fortunate
as we had a high river and this meant we would make
wonderfully good time.  We sighted two rafts quite a
way up the river, floating down.  We didn't see any
ahead of us.

We were gone but a short time when I noticed my
father getting very active.  As our raft was about 120
feet long with a width of some twenty-five feet, he had
a responsibility on his hands.  We were entering the
narrow channel below Bushkill with very swift water
and some dangerous rocks in the channel.  As a heavy
log raft took at least a foot and one-half of water, it
was necessary to avoid any rock that didn't have two

feet of water pouring over it.

In order for the two front oarsmen to obey his orders, my father used his arms as well as his voice; for the Pennsylvania side he held out his right arm and for Jersey his left. To signal for "hold" he held his arms straight up.

The raft had gained speed and we were shooting along at a rapid pace, the rocks towering up on both sides and large boulders sticking out of the water, some with water pouring over them. I marvel now how they managed to get those huge rafts through such rifts without an accident, but in no time we were opposite Wallpack Bend and entering Sambo and Mary Rift. We shot through that and then they called to my brother and me to "watch for VanCamp's Nose." Sure enough, on the right side we passed a large rock sticking out of the water, the shape of a man's nose. Before we knew it we were passing Heller-Dimmick Ferry and as we neared Tock's Island we looked back up the river and counted seven rafts.

We went through Walters' Eddy and Trach's Eddy and in a short time were down to Walker's Ferry at Shawnee. As we entered to go down back of Muskrat Island I looked across and could see our house and barn. Many a day we youngsters stood up by "the post" as we called it, right near our home, where we had a wonderful view of the Delaware and could watch and count the rafts going down the river   right where our raft was at that time. I wish I could describe in words the feeling it gave me   one of the highlights of the trip.

We soon sighted the New York, Susquehanna and Western Railroad bridge and I noticed my father was getting very active again. The piers under the bridge were quite close together for a large raft; also the rift right below the bridge caused a current and there was a strong wind blowing. He had to take all these things into consideration. I noticed the oarsmen were watching him very closely. Well, we went sailing through under that bridge and then the rift, which I later learned was a dangerous one as the current tended to throw the raft to Jersey and the oarsmen had to work to keep the raft from hitting the rocks along the shore. We were really going and to this day I get a thrill thinking about it. Then through the Delaware Water Gap on a raft. My, those mountains seemed high to me. Well, there wasn't a dull moment.

We entered the rift just below the Gap and in no time sighted the old Portland covered bridge--again a narrow place to pilot a raft between the stone piers. A swift flowing rift just below Portland, and then in one-half hour we were nearing Foul Rift about one mile below Belvidere the most treacherous rift of any in the Delaware, with the greatest drop. More rafts "stove up" (i.e., broke up) in Foul Rift than any place on the river. Years ago the government spent considerable money to make the river navigable for boats and rafts, and as you pass through Foul Rift you can still see dynamite holes in the rocks along the shore.

As we sighted the rift my father told us to stay on top of the store box and keep our feet up on the box. Well, even though I was twelve years old, I noticed the men at the oars were watching my father very closely. He was looking straight ahead, giving orders with his hands and arms. The roar of the water was such that the men couldn't hear his voice. I can see that rift just as it looked that day. The river being very high, it seemed as though we just shot along. The roar of the water was indescribable. Half way through, where there is a sudden drop in the river, the front of the raft dove under, causing about eighteen inches of water to come over the logs. I knew then why my father nailed that store box to the logs and why he told us to keep our feet on top of the box.

We were through the rift in no time and all was peaceful and calm again. In about one-half hour we entered Saundt's Eddy   very deep water and no drop or fall in the river for a distance of five miles. For the first time the raft didn't make over three miles an hour. Half way through the eddy my father called "Pennsylvania," and the men pulled the raft to shore. They threw out the ropes, tied up the raft and he said, "Now you boys get out on shore, run around and get some exercise. The men have one hour rest and we will go up and get our dinner." It was a farmhouse and they served meals to the raftsmen. It was one o'clock, meaning that the men had stood at those oars for six hours and most of the time busy. In a short time more rafts were landing back of us and my father seemed to know all the steersmen. What a time they had visiting and telling about things that had happened on the trip. Some of the rafts had been two and three days on the way, coming from up in York State on the East and West branches of the Delaware.

My brother and I got lots of attention as we were the only boys on any of the rafts.

We left at two o'clock and my father said we would reach Easton at five and get the six o'clock Pennsylvania train home. When we finally pulled out in the current again I don't know how many rafts were tied up for dinner and more coming. Some of them didn't stop so we now had rafts ahead of us and in the rear also. When we got to Easton we could see both Jersey and Pennsylvania shores were lined with rafts. We pulled in at the first opening, and by the time my father finished his arrangements for selling the raft it was train time. My uncle met us at the Delaware Water Gap station with the three-seated wagon but I never woke up until we reached home.

The importance of lumbering and rafting in the economy of the nineteenth century farm should not be overlooked. As I mentioned earlier, nearly every back woods farmer did some lumbering and many ran at least one raft during a season. Farming was only a side line; the hay and grass they raised to partly feed their working cattle; for getting out logs and running sawmills was their profitable business. It was the timber trade that brought prosperity to many an early farm. The combined lumbering and farming operations of J.D. and Hiram LeBar, spanning the period 1830-1890, were thus typical of that time.

Sometimes log rafts were run right through to city markets but generally they stopped at "selling eddies" such as Easton. There were many lumber mills along the Delaware below Easton, places such as

Lumberton, Lumberville and the like. The last of these mills in the Easton area was built around 1860. They were usually located where a stream or river entered the main channel, since these mills depended to a large extent on back country trade for their existence. By the 1880's these mills had mostly shut down or converted to other uses, due largely to deforestation on the upper Delaware and to competition from railroads for the back country trade. By 1910 the Lumberville mill was the only one of these early river mills still operating.

East Stroudsburg State Normal School

Stroudsburg Woolen Mill, Thomas Kitson, Owner

Advertisement for Eilenberger Mills

A log raft steered down the Delaware river by Harry LeBar, built at Dingmans, and landed at Minisink Hills, Pennsylvania, in the Spring of 1902. Pictured, left to right: Fred Eilenberger, C.B Eilenberger, Judge C.B. Staples, Judge of Monroe County, and William Eilenberger

LeBar & Michaels Feed and Grain Store, 1913, located on lower Main Street, Stroudsburg, with the Erie Railroad tracks visible to the right.  Pictured, left to right: Ed Pugh, Elmer Chambers, Frank LeBar, and Tom Heller

LeBar's Drug Store, Stroudsburg,
owned by Amzi "Uncle Doc" LeBar

Omar Michaels farm about 1905.  The Trach farm, site of
Hialeah Park, is in the distance

Minisink Avenue, 1905.  Advertisement, Minisink Land
Company, Webster Eilenberger, President

# EIGHT

# THE END OF AN ERA

The village of Shawnee changed very little from the time that I can remember until the year 1898. In the spring of that year news spread through the village that C.C. Worthington, owner of the Worthington Pump Company, in New York City, had purchased the Charles Smith farm located in New Jersey one mile above Shawnee. My great-great- grandfather, Daniel LeBar, Jr., acquired this same farm in 1804 and both my father and grandfather were born there. The property consisted of about one hundred fifty acres of land, with an old stone house and barn. The Worthington interests also bought the O'Brien farm just south of the Smith farm. The former comprised some forty acres, mostly woodland, with a house located on the mountain side.

The rumor was that the Worthingtons would tear down the O'Brien home and build a hunting lodge, with stables for horses. All Shawnee was excited and rumors of further changes began to circulate. Work started at once and the lodge was completed by fall. I think it was in October on a Friday afternoon that we heard a horn echo through the village and down the Shawnee Hill came the Worthington tallyho drawn by four horses. A three-seated carriage loaded with guests followed the coach. They crossed the river at Walker's Ferry and proceeded to the lodge on the mountainside. This was something new and strange for the quiet little village of Shawnee.

From then on there was activity. We heard the Worthingtons had bought the Marshall Walker farm and the Walker Ferry and that the latter would be discontinued. One farm after another was purchased, also the mountain side beginning at the Pahaquarry copper mine and continuing down to the Far View Hotel (now Karamac Inn). The news was that this entire area would be enclosed by a high fence and stocked with deer. The fence was finished the following year and the enclosed area stocked with one hundred deer. In the fall of 1900 C.C. Worthington organized his first deer hunt, inviting fifteen or twenty friends to the lodge. They hired men from around Shawnee to drive the deer. [*Much of this acreage is included in the present Worthington State Park.*]

In 1898 my father decided that my brother John and I should attend the Model School, or grade school, at that time connected with the East Stroudsburg State Normal School. Classes were taught by Normal School seniors about to get their teaching certificates. We walked to school and back each day    five miles one way. If it rained we drove Old Frog, our horse, and stayed all night at Aunt Belle Knapp's or with Aunt Bertha Peters, sisters of my mother. Some twelve or fourteen  young people regularly walked to school, three from Minisink Hills and six or seven from the Delaware Water Gap. The three from Minisink would meet us at Eilenberger's mill and those from Delaware Water Gap usually caught up with us near the Paper Mill.

When winter set in we drove Old Frog, hooked to the gun boat. This was an old sleigh that had belonged to my grandfather, Judge Depue LeBar. The date painted on the back was 1790. The sleigh was wide, so that three people could sit on the back seat comfortably and two or three youngsters could cuddle down in the front. We had a buffalo robe on the floor, making the sleigh warm and cozy. It was the only one of its kind anywhere around and attracted much attention. It was later purchased at the sale of our family effects by Purdy Cope, then owner and manager of the Kittatinny Hotel. He paid a handsome price for it and had it on display in front of the hotel. When the Kittatinny burned, the sleigh, stored inside the building, was destroyed.

On those walks back and forth to the East Stroudsburg State Normal School we had many exciting experiences. In the spring of 1899 (March 20th) it started to snow about eleven a.m. By the time school let out at three-thirty it had turned into a blizzard, snowing and blowing so that we could hardly see. I was going to walk to Aunt Bertha's alone but John said, "No, Ben, I'm going to walk with you," and I was glad he went along. We could hardly see the road and the drifts were already bad. The blizzard continued all night and when we got up in the morning everything was drifted shut. I remember Uncle Phil Peters had difficulty shoveling a path to his barn. The roads were all drifted shut as they had no snow fences in those days.

There was no telephone to Shawnee and our parents had no way of knowing whether we had started home or not. My father put a saddle on one of our work horses and started on horseback to find us. In those days they simply took to the fields wherever the roads were drifted shut. He found us at Aunt Bertha's and after resting he said to John, "I'll take you with me, but Ben, you will have to stay here." Well, he could see how disappointed I was and so he promised he would come back the next day and get me. As I watched them leaving, everything went out from under me and I was just sick. Uncle Phil played checkers and dominoes with me and they did everything they could think of. I couldn't eat or sleep.

In the morning there wasn't a thing to see but snow. As I watched the road all I could think of was my father's promise; and sure enough about 1 p.m. I saw Old Frog and the gun boat coming. I grabbed my cap and ran out and I think my father knew how glad I was to see him. When I reached home my mother was so nice to me: "Never mind about it Ben, you will never be homesick again." And I never was.

\* \* \* \*

In the fall of 1899 my brother entered Nazareth Hall Military School, where he remained two years. In the fall of 1902 my parents decided to send me to the East Stroudsburg State Normal School for a two-year course in preparation for college. I boarded at the school, but went home quite often on weekends, always taking a classmate with me. Ernest Roselle was my close friend and consequently went home with me quite often.

The East Stroudsburg State Normal School [now East Stroudsburg University] was founded in 1896. When it was decided to build a school there was difficulty in raising the money, the State finally agreeing to furnish half and the citizens the balance. My mother gave most of the land where the college is now located, and my father gave some $2,000 toward the buildings. The year I graduated, 1904, I was elected President of the Alumni Association, and later served as a member of the Board of Trustees.

In the spring of 1903 I was called home due to the death of my mother. Then on a Friday in early October my father phoned me to come home as the Delaware was rising fast. The roads were already flooded and I would have to come by way of the Paper Mill, following the NYS&W Railroad tracks past the Minisink Hills Church, then cutting back to the main road again. I couldn't believe my eyes when I saw the Paper Mill under water, the DL&W Railroad tracks, Fred Eilenberger's lumber yard, saw mill, and so on   all under water. But the big surprise came when I reached the top of Shawnee Hill and could look down into the valley   a sea of water from the Jersey mountain to the foothills in Pennsylvania. The big (Shawnee) island was completely under water. My father had eighty acres of corn in shock and thirty acres of winter wheat and I realized all this would be a total loss. Our two barns on the island were gone, together with forty tons of hay, our new binder, mowing machine, roller, cultivators, harrows, plows and so on   all gone. When I reached home the water was up to our porch, in fact our four boats were tied there. The barn was partially flooded and they had put all the stock in an enclosure above the highway. My father was deeply depressed as he visualized his prize farm in ruins.

On Sunday morning the flood reached its crest and my father said to me, "Ben, let's take a boat, row out and catch some of the boats floating down the river." Despite a cold, drizzling rain we went out and caught three or four nice boats which we pulled to shore. Then we saw a two-story house come floating down the river. It lodged against two walnut trees, about 15 feet apart, which stood about where Shawnee Inn is now. When the river went down we of course explored the house. Four rooms down and four up, downstairs covered with mud, but upstairs three bedrooms the beds nicely made and no damage done. The house belonged to Bill Schoonover of Bushkill, and in the spring he came with teams and wagons, took it apart and hauled it back to Bushkill.

I returned to school but by the following Friday my father was fatally ill with pneumonia. With his passing, October 25, 1903, we all realized that our lives were about to change. We were saddened, too, by the thought that he had to live to see his lovely farm in ruins. My eldest brother Harry came home from the West and we decided to rent the farm in the spring. Harry was fortunate in getting one of the best farmers in the county, Oliver Michaels, to take over the farm April 1, 1904. We held an auction sale in March, selling all livestock, machinery, and household goods. It was a two-day sale, Friday and Saturday; Reeder Posten (father of Wayne Posten) and John Frederick were the auctioneers. I got home for one day, Saturday, and by evening everything was gone. It was a great adjustment for all of us. Within a year the remaining members of our family were widely scattered; five of the eight children eventually made their home in the western United States. Only two, my sister Alma and myself, were to remain permanently in the area where for 100 years our ancestors had lived and farmed along the Delaware.

Our family farm and homestead was subsequently acquired in 1908 by the C.C. Worthington estate, which continued for some time to purchase property in and around Shawnee. In 1911 the Worthingtons built Buckwood Inn and golf course on what had been my father's farm.

# FROM FARM TO MILL: THE MAKING OF A BUSINESSMAN

Following the death of both parents in 1903, we children arranged to rent the family farm and also sold off the household effects at auction, as previously stated. Just before the sale my older sister, Alma, my brothers Paul and Carl, and I moved to a house (the former Tommy Cullen property) on Minisink Avenue in Shawnee. This was the first house built by the Minisink Land Company, Webster Eilenberger, president. The company laid out building lots along the former Walker Ferry Lane which was renamed Minisink Avenue. My father had purchased this house just a few months before he passed away.

My marks in higher mathematics at the East Stroudsburg Normal School were averaging over ninety percent and as a result Professor Higley encouraged me to apply for entrance to Stevens Institute of Surveying and Mining Engineering. I was accepted and expected to enter Stevens after graduation but my father's death changed these plans. The estate would not be settled for a year; Stevens was an expensive school and I did not have the money. I decided then to try teaching school for a year. Following graduation in 1904, I was elected teacher of the Shawnee School, to open in September. In the meantime I had three months to spend with my sister and brothers in our temporary home on Minisink Avenue. I asked Oliver Michaels, who was then renting and operating our farm, if I could have land for a garden. He plowed a nice piece of land and we young folks planted it and practically lived off that vegetable garden that summer.

Oliver Michaels had a daughter Grace, dark wavy hair, brown eyes, and very nice. I invited her to take a ride to Bushkill on a Sunday afternoon. We stopped for an ice cream soda and reached home just before a thunder storm. Her father said I should unhook my horse, put him in the stable, and come in for supper. It was just like going back home. Mother Michaels made me feel at ease and her mustard pickles tasted just like my mother's. The Shawnee Sunday School picnic was held that year at Saylor's Lake and William

Heller, my uncle, drove a three-seated wagon, twelve miles each way. Grace and I sat on the back seat, not too well acquainted. But after spending the day with her, getting home about nine p.m., I knew I had met the girl who was going to be my partner, providing she was willing. We spent a lovely day together and have enjoyed one another's company since that day fifty-three years ago.

My brothers and sisters and I, as heirs to my father's estate, managed to keep his driving horse, Duke, and his rubber tired buggy. He had had this buggy made to order by Blum Brothers, wagon builders in Scranton. It had a wide seat covered with red plush and was a beautiful wagon. We were lucky to have a horse and buggy and enjoyed it to the full. On Saturday evenings I would harness Duke  wagon all shined up  pick up Miss Michaels and we would drive to Stroudsburg. Tied old Duke to a hitching post on Main Street. We would have a dish of ice cream or a soda, then sit in the wagon and listen to the Stroudsburg band. In the summer they held a concert on Main Street every Saturday evening. Then we would take our time driving home, often with a full moon shining down. What could have been more enjoyable? Some may poke fun now at the horse and buggy days, but we rode along perfectly relaxed, no horns blowing behind us. We tied our horse to a hitching post  no dime in a meter and no rushing back for fear of getting a parking ticket. Well, I am glad we lived to enjoy the "horse and buggy days." As well as I can remember, we accomplished almost everything we wanted and I believe we lived a normal life.

The summer of 1904 passed all too quickly and on September 8th I was ready to start my first job, teaching the one-room Shawnee school (total thirty-five scholars). I was at the school building at eight o'clock in the morning, opened the window, swept the floor and got things in order. I knew most of the pupils as I had grown up with them. They included my two brothers, Paul and Carl, my sister Aura, and Russell Michaels, my future brother-in-law. It was his first year in school and I can see him now as he walked in that schoolroom, dressed as neat as a pin. I assigned him the front seat on the boy's side. Well, nine o'clock arrived, I rang the bell and school opened. The first day was spent in giving out the books, registering each pupil, giving each one pencil and paper, filling the ink wells, one in each desk, and assigning lessons for the following day. Every Friday afternoon we had a spelling bee, four divisions, A, B, C, and D. Each division in turn was called up to the front, standing in a line. Those who misspelled a word had to sit down and the last one standing was given a credit card. Prizes were awarded at the end of the year. After the spelling bee we had recitations, reading and singing. The pupils enjoyed this and it taught them to speak in public.

When school closed that year Dr. Kemp offered me a position as principal of a graded school in Kane, Pennsylvania, at a salary of $100 per month. I thanked him but made some excuse. The real reason was that school teaching as a profession did not interest me. I took a temporary position with Fred Eilenberger at Minisink Hills. He wanted a bookkeeper and secretary for his lumber and feed mills. I started work one week after school closed and my first job was counting lumber. He had placed a saw mill on the bank of the Delaware where Camp Wyomissing is now. There he had ten log rafts that had been rafted down the river from Bushkill. My brother, Harry LeBar, was steersman on two of these, having learned the technique from my father. They were hemlock logs, and my job was to count the board feet of lumber as it came down from the mill. I kept a record of 2x4x10 feet, 2x6x10 feet, and so on. The logs ran in lengths from 10, 12, 14, 16, 20 feet, and were sawed into boards of various sizes. At the end of the day I had a record of the amount of lumber sawed, different sizes, and so on. After six weeks I was transferred to the office, where I kept the books for the lumber yard, planning mill, grist mill, and cider mill. The cider mill was the only one in the Shawnee area. It made cider three days a week. Teams and wagons loaded with apples    four barrels on the top of each load    would line up awaiting their turn. It took about twenty minutes per wagon load to grind, press and fill the barrels. We received five cents a gallon for the work involved, amounting to about $12 per wagon.

I stayed with Fred Eilenberger about five months, learning something about lumber and the flour and feed business. On October 1st, 1905, I accepted a position as bookkeeper and teller with the Monroe County National Bank of East Stroudsburg. I thought it would be well to learn something of the banking business, although I had no idea of making it a career. In those days a young man going in a bank as bookkeeper or teller was resigned to a long wait for someone to die before he could be advanced. I posted deposits and charges on all accounts and acted as teller for two hours a day. No adding machines in those days and you did your own adding and subtracting in posting the ledgers.

In the spring I asked Frank Michaels and Clinton B. Eilenberger to let me know if they heard of any business opening around Stroudsburg. In July Frank Michaels informed me that Thomas J. Kitson's secretary was leaving and there would be a vacancy for secretary of the Thomas J. Kitson and Son's Woolen Mills. I was getting $60 per month at the bank; the Kitson position would start at $88.88 and I would soon be getting $100 per month   good pay in 1906. Mr. Kitson set a date to stop in his office for an interview. I had never met him, and found a man about fifty years old, an Englishman, very stern. I could see he was a man who gave orders and expected them to be carried out. He wanted me to start working September first, 1906, hours seven a.m. to 5:45 p.m. I gave up my position at the bank and went to Philadelphia for a three-week course in accounting at the Pierce Business School. I was glad I took this course as keeping books for a large industry was complicated; but I had no trouble, with the knowledge I gained at Philadelphia.

I reported to work September first and found Mr. Kitson a gentleman in every way, ready to show me anything I didn't understand. I was lucky to have a good stenographer, Sadie Bittenbender MacDonald, who knew about making up the payroll, ordering supplies for the mill, keeping records of outgoing cloth, and records of inventory of raw material. For some two months I worked nights until I learned the details of the business.

Employees were paid in gold and silver; during the seven years I was with the Woolen Mill I never used a paper bill in paying. Even Mr. Kitson himself took his salary in ten ten-dollar gold pieces every two weeks. The payroll averaged from six to seven thousand dollars. I had a heavy steel box which the liveryman would take to the Stroudsburg National Bank on a Friday morning. I would give the bank the number of five and ten dollar gold pieces, the number of wagon wheels (silver dollars) and the number of fifty cent pieces, quarters, dimes, and so on. The box when filled weighed about seventy-five pounds. I would be at the bank about one o'clock. Mr Kitson's liveryman, Emmett Hallet, would get the box, put it on the wagon, drive me down to the mill and remain in the room while I put the money in envelopes. Every employee had a number, together with his or her name, on an envelope. They would march by a small window in the hallway and I would pass out their envelopes. They came in order starting with number one and going on to 350. Emmett Hallet had a gun on his hip and we never had any trouble. In the spring of the year the mill would buy all the wool raised in Monroe County, and it seemed as though every farmer kept a few sheep. They would bring their wool in, take it to the wool shed where it was weighed and where they were given a credit slip. They would bring the slip up to me and I would give them a check. In this way I learned to know many of the farmers in Monroe County. This acquaintance was of much help to me when I later started my own flour and feed business.

* * * * *

On September 21, 1907, Grace Michaels and I were married in her home in Shawnee, which had also been my home. The living room in which we were married I had known for nineteen years, and that room held many fond memories. The Rev. Porter Dalrymple performed the ceremony.

I stayed with the woolen mill six years with only one vacation   the week I took off to get married. In 1912 I finally decided I was going to stop working for someone else. I immediately began looking around and found a flour and feed business for sale on lower Main Street. The owner was my brother-in-law, Burton Michaels, and I operated the business initially as LeBar and Michaels until 1914 when I was able to buy out his share. The mill was well located, had the best of machinery for grinding and mixing dairy and chicken feeds, and had a siding on the NYS&W railroad tracks for loading and unloading feed, flour and grain.

Selling was my hobby and I knew a good market existed if I could give service and quality. I told Mr. Kitson I was going in business and wanted to start operations October first. He said he admired any young man who wanted to strike out for himself and would give me all his trade, which would be considerable. I discovered that grain, feed and flour came sight draft, which meant I had to pay before I could unload a car. At that time a car of flour cost $1200, a car of corn $800, a car of wheat $1600, a car of oats $700. I intended to give thirty days credit on bills, and by paying cash for all grain to start I would need about $18,000. And I didn't have this amount of money.

Frank Michaels was cashier and P.R. Johnson, who owned the Glenwood Hotel, was president of the Security Trust Co. Mr. Johnson was also a close friend of my family. I sat down with these two men, told them my story, and they agreed to take up the proposition with the bank board, which would meet the next day. They called me after the meeting, said to come up to the bank. Of course I was quite nervous. They told me the board had granted me a loan up to and not exceeding $18,000. The bank would want a note covering everything in my mill, also my credit accounts. I expected this and agreed one hundred percent. I have never to this day forgotten how much I owe Frank Michaels for his confidence in me.

The first thing was to buy a team of horses and a delivery wagon. I knew I must have a first class miller, one who understood his job. I was most fortunate in getting Elmer Chambers, the miller in a large feed mill in Scranton.  As his home was in Stroudsburg he was glad to get the position in his home town.  I paid him good money but he knew his business, was honest, a hard worker, and he stayed with me until I sold the mill.  I hired a girl who had completed her high school commercial course to be in charge of the office, hired a driver for the delivery wagon, a helper in the mill. Then I wrote a letter, including quotations on horse, chicken and dairy feeds as well as bread and pastry flour, and ordered seven or eight carloads of grain, flour and the like.  I was fortunate in getting Charlie Pugh and his son, Ed, to load and unload all cars. Wheat, corn and oats came loose, 1000 to 1200 bushels to a car.  All dairy feeds, bran, cottonseed oil meal, beet pulp, brewer's grains   in fact all feeds came in one-hundred pound bags.  Charlie and Ed handled those heavy bags all day and it never bothered them.

I first contacted Mr. Truslow, who owned a duck farm in South Stroudsburg  He raised ducks for market, never under 20,000, and ducks do little but eat.  He gave me his business, worth one hundred dollars a day, and paid me within thirty to sixty days. Then I contacted Guillot Brothers at Bushkill.  They had 5000 chickens and gave me all their business, as did the Shawna Poultry Farm in Shawnee, owned by C.C. Worthington and managed by a Mr. Martin; they kept 10,000 chickens, the largest poultry farm in the area.

By spring my trade had increased to the point that I needed more storage room. I couldn't keep the merchandise on hand to fill the orders. My miller estimated we needed space to take care of at least twenty carloads of feed, flour and the like. I asked Mr. Strunk of Delaware Water Gap, who traded with me and was a good carpenter, to give me a figure on building a three-story addition to the rear of the mill, to be attached to the existing structure  thus saving me the cost of an extra wall. No cellar and a board roof covered with asbestos tar paper. By doing the work with the help of one man he built it for $2800. I had a long lease and the owner agreed to the construction, so I was safe in putting up the addition and paying for it. It was well I built it when I did as we used all the space and it permitted me to increase my volume of business considerably.

The building was finished May first, and I was ready to go after more business. William Mackey of Blairstown, New Jersey, operated a large livery stable, renting out horses and wagons, also riding horses to Blair Academy. He kept about twenty horses and was buying all his feed, hay and straw from me. He talked me into the idea of driving around the country within a radius of twenty miles of Blairstown and contacting dairy farmers. He knew most of the farmers and dairymen in the area. Well, I took the New York, Susquehanna and Western Railroad, leaving Stroudsburg at five a.m. Got to Blairstown at six o'clock, where Bill Mackey had two fast horses and a buggy ready. We drove all day and visited thirty or more dairy farms. Had dinner at Newton, returning to

Blairstown in time for me to catch the 6:50 train home to Stroudsburg.  I came back with orders to fill two cars   forty tons of various kinds of cow feed   a fine day's work.  After this I went to Blairstown every two weeks; Bill Mackey would see new customers for me and I built up a fine business.  By this time I had registered my own brands of dairy feed, chicken feed and horse feed.  We mixed and ground all these brands ourselves.

Well, Bill Mackey wanted me to see the headmaster of Blair Academy, Dr. Sharp, who had a large dairy (forty to sixty thoroughbred cattle), around 6000 chickens and a number of horses. Bill was sure I could persuade Dr. Sharp to let me supply him with his feed requirements. I made an appointment to meet him in his office, told him why I had come and he said, "Mr. LeBar, I have a mill of my own right here in Blairstown and hire a miller. Wouldn't I be foolish to buy feed of you?" I replied that he would indeed unless I could save him money and give him quality feed and service. I then gave him my quotations, which were cheaper than he was paying his own miller. He gave me a trial order, asking me to come back in two weeks. I then received another trial order, and Dr. Sharp finally asked me if I would supply him with all his feeds; he figured his requirements would run around $40,000 a year. If I would ship to Blairstown, carload lots, pay the draft checks and oversee everything, he would pay me every thirty days and add five percent for my commission. I agreed, and furnished him all his feeds until the day I sold the business. I never dealt with a finer man.

As of October first, 1913, I had been in business one year and was operating the mill at capacity. My door trade alone kept one man busy  farmers coming in to buy their dairy feed, chicken feed, flour, chicken utensils of all kind, poultry and horse medicines and powders, chick feed, oyster shells, bailed hay and straw, and so on. I had also added a four-ton truck and a one-ton truck, selling the team and wagon, so we could cover more territory on our deliveries.

\*  \*  \*  \*  \*

In 1912 Lewis Pipher opened a garage across from my feed mill and handled the Krit car. He had started with a bicycle business at Minisink Hills, and by the year 1903 had the first automobile in the county. He would drive it up to the Shawnee store and give us rides. These were usually short, however, as the roads were rough and very dusty in the summertime. He had difficulty getting up the Shawnee Hill; would get a good start, driving with all the speed he had, but the outlets ("thank-you-mams") across the road slowed him down and we would have to hook our team in front of his car and help him up.

Well, in the spring of 1913 Lew talked me into buying a Krit. In those days we needed no driver's license and took no examination. Lew took me up North Fifth Street where I took the wheel, learned to turn around and steer. We went back to the garage and Lew said he would be around at noon and let me drive it home. Come noon and Lew wasn't there, the car was standing in front of his garage and it was time for me to leave. I went over, looked at the car, said to his man, "Start it up and I'll drive home." As I approached our house on Fulmer Avenue I blew the horn and it was then I realized I didn't know how to stop the car. Well, I went right on around the block. I got rather panicky, didn't dare to take my eyes off the road, so I kept feeling around on the dash board. I got to our house again, waved my hand, and went right on. Then I discovered there was a button which had to be pushed in before starting the car and pulled out to disconnect and stop it. When I came around again I pulled up in front of the house and stopped.

The following year we decided to drive to Atlantic City, leaving Saturday morning and returning home Monday. I took the car to Lew Pipher, told him to go all over it as we were taking a trip. He checked it and said we would have no trouble. Well, we left Stroudsburg on Saturday morning. The roads were rough and dusty   no concrete highways in those days. We went by way of Nazareth, Bethlehem and Allentown. Between Bethlehem and Allentown we were riding along enjoying ourselves when we hit a rut, something cracked, and the rods holding our windshield snapped, letting the windshield fall on the hood of the car. The top went with it and there we sat with no windshield and no top. At that time there were very few garages; the blacksmith shops fixed cars. Luck was with us as a nearby shop welded the two rods back in place and we were on our way.

As we took the turnpike from Bethlehem to Philadelphia we hit a rough piece of road, something cracked again, and down went the side of the car. We again looked for a blacksmith shop and found that the frame underneath one side of the car had broken in half. Well, I asked the blacksmith what could be done. He thought for a time, then said he had a piece of narrow gauge railroad iron, said he would jack the car up, shove the iron through underneath, and wire it fast to both axles. Said he was sure it would work. Sure enough, the car seemed as good as ever and we proceeded on our way. We visited Atlantic City, drove up and down the coast and then started for home. Had two flat tires, but in those days we thought nothing of that.

As we neared Mount Bethel and were going down Three Church Hill, the front side of the car dropped down and I saw our front wheel preceding us down the street. It continued on down the hill and bounced up on someone's front porch, where it finally came to rest. Well, we got that fixed and arrived home at last after a fine weekend trip. But I decided to get rid of the Krit car, the sooner the better. I traded it on a new seven passenger Hudson, which as I remember cost $1100. That car made it possible to give pleasure to many people, and we were happy when we had all seven seats filled.

We knew nothing of taxicabs in those days and anyone could take passengers in his car and charge for it. Charlie Ross had a seven passenger car the same as mine and he was taking guests from

Buckwood Inn for rides and charging them.  He had more business than he could handle and asked me if I would like to help out.  I asked him what he charged and he told me $10 per hour and that the guests usually took a two-hour ride.  It sounded like a lot of money to me so I asked him to make the necessary arrangements.  About a week later he called and had a party (man and wife) for a two-hour drive.  I was to be at the Inn door at three p.m.  I should say that this was a completely new experience for me.  The only people I had ever taken for a drive were friends, and by the time the trip was over I had learned a lot.  I drove up to the front door, told the doorman a party of two were looking for me.  He found the couple, came out with them, opened my back door, they got in.  I noticed that they were probably about sixty years of age.  They took no notice of me, but I thought nothing of it.

It was a beautiful day in late August, warm but the wind was blowing a gale.  As we drove over the open stretch between the hotel and Shawnee Hall a sudden gust caught my straw hat and away it went.  I stopped the car, looked at my passengers and made a remark about it being a bad time for my hat to blow off.  They never cracked a smile or said a word.  As we drove by my old home I remarked, "My father owned this house and all the land where the hotel stands."  No comment.  When we got to the top of the hill and could look down on the island and golf course, I said my father had owned that land and all the land bordering on the road.  No comment.  As we drove through the Water Gap we passed the Kittatinny Hotel.  Purdy Cope, the owner, had bought an old sleigh at our sale and mounted it on a concrete platform in front of the hotel. As we passed by I remarked, "That old sleigh belonged to my father." Still no comment from the back seat. I then realized they must think me the biggest liar they had ever met.

We crossed the Portland bridge, drove to what is now Karamac Inn, turned around, drove back to Buckwood Inn and up to the front door. The man said, "How much do we owe you?" I told him and he handed me a $20 bill. The only words they spoke on the entire trip were to tell me where to drive. Well, when he handed me the money I was so disgusted I didn't even thank him. As I drove home I thought, "Here is a couple who have all the money they want, but to my knowledge that beautiful drive meant nothing to them. I may not have much money but at least I enjoy the simple things of life." That trip had thrilled me many times and I wanted to say "Oh look at that, and that, and that," but I had learned to keep quiet and not even turn my head.

When I reached Stroudsburg I stopped at the mill. Elmer Chambers, my miller, said, "Well, Frank, how did you make out with your city boarders?" I told him that was my first trip out for money and my last. He laughed and laughed: "I knew one trip was all you would make. You like your work here, talking with farmers, dairymen, lumbermen, and helping wait on customers when you have time." And he summed it up about right.

By this time I had paid off my loans at the bank, paid the mortgage on my home, and had a bank balance. I was thankful for this as the first World War had started and we were beginning to feel its effects. Prices of all grains were going up. Scattergood and Company, large grain merchants in Philadelphia, advised me to keep well stocked as freight cars were getting scarce and much wheat, corn and flour going to Europe. My miller had every space filled to the roof and all our bins were filled with grain. Conditions continued to worsen, and when we entered the war in 1917 flour was immediately rationed and ration books distributed. We could sell one hundred pounds of flour to a customer but they had to buy twenty pounds of corn meal and twenty pounds of oatmeal with it. People began making mush and baking oatmeal bread.

I began spending more of my time at the mill as there were arguments about giving out flour. I had at least three carloads on hand and the bakers were all after me to let them have flour, price no object. I let two of them have a stipulated amount each week but I wanted to keep enough for my customers. People began hoarding flour and one had to keep a cool head and use the best of judgment in dealing it out. It wasn't long before our stock of everything began getting low. The government had priority on the railroads, in fact the government took them over and ran them until the war ended. I had large stocks of feed in transit, but as there were no airplanes or trucking companies the railroads had to haul everything. I could sell anything I had on hand, the trouble was to replace it. I even had grain shipped in on the DL&W and hauled it over from East Stroudsburg by truck.

Then came the fall of 1918 and the flu epidemic. I happened to be among the first to come down sick with it. In addition to these difficulties I was getting competition, plenty of it. A cooperative mill had opened in East Stroudsburg, one at Snydersville and one at Broadheadsville. The Flory Company, a large milling operation in Bangor, had opened branch mills in Portland, Wind Gap and Nazareth, and were looking for a location in Stroudsburg. Mr. Flory called for an appointment and wanted to buy my business. There were already rumors that the New York, Susquehanna and Western Railroad was going to abandon its line from Stroudsburg to Blairstown, and this would leave my mill without a railroad siding. I would have to haul everything from the DL&W station in East Stroudsburg. Mr. Flory was willing to pay me cash, pay the market price for goods on hand, take my two trucks and keep all my help. Well, I was doing a fine business but I knew automobiles were coming in rapidly, also trucks. Horses were disappearing, so I would lose that business. After thinking it over from all angles I agreed to sell. The NYS&W abandoned their road within two years, so I was fortunate in selling when I did.

I enjoyed my seven years in the flour and feed business. I was fortunate to be in a line that was not competitive at the time. This was changing rapidly, however, as stores all over the country began to handle chicken feed, as the horse feed business became a thing of the past, as women stopped baking bread at home, and as the larger mills began opening chain outlets in every community.

\* \* \* \*

In the spring of 1919 I entered into partnership with William L'Hommedieu selling real estate. The firm of LeBar and L'Hommedieu continued business at 554 Main Street in Stroudsburg until 1932. As the earliest real estate and investment brokers in the Stroudsburgs we witnessed the transition of Monroe County in the decade following World War I    the growth of industry and the increasing importance of summer resorts, as the County became tied ever closer to the metropolitan centers of New York and Philadelphia. I like to think that Will L'Hommedieu and I, as pioneer real estate brokers in the area, played a role in this growth and development. We were the first to develop land and sell off lots at auction, and in 1922 we purchased the Trach farm one mile above Shawnee and laid out the lots for what became Hialeah Park [*the present DWGNRA Hialeah picnic ground*]. Early owners of these lots and their summer cottages facing the river were, beginning at the lower end of the Park: Harry Allen, Frank LeBar, Dr. Roland Collins, Stanley Howell, A. J. Zabriskie, William. L'Hommedieu, Dr. L. E. Ace, and Ernest H. Wyckoff.

In the year 1910 John J. Newberry and family moved to Stroudsburg and located on Scott Street. He had been with Kress 5 and 10 cent stores, but resigned his position with them and came to Stroudsburg to regain his health. He felt so much better by 1911 that he decided to start a chain of stores for himself. He bought out the Jacob Ruster Variety store, located next to the Stroudsburg National Bank and opened his first store. Will and I helped him in financing the store. By 1923 he had twenty-one stores operating. He then decided to move his offices to N. Y. City and incorporate as the J.J. Newberry Company. He issued $1,000,000 of stock and gave Will and me the privilege of selling it, we to receive stock in the company for our commission. As Will ran the office, I spent all of my time out selling the stock. Altogether I sold $1,000,000 worth. The Newberrys were born in Wilkes-Barre and C.T. Newberry, who lived in Wilkes-Barre, had become a partner with John. The family was well known in that section and known as very successful businessmen. I spent many weeks in selling the stock in and around Wilkes-Barre and placed $500,000 of the stock with different investors in that area. I thoroughly enjoyed the work as I made many fine friends, and they all gave me names of people who would be interested in buying the stock. I sold the other $500,000 in Monroe County and surrounding country.

After 1932 I continued in the real estate and investment security business alone, and later with the assistance of Forrest H. Smith. During the 1930's and 1940's I bought and sold properties throughout the County, specializing in farm and lake properties. Sales I particularly remember included Buckwood Inn (now Shawnee Inn), The Ontwood and other hotels and boarding houses in the Poconos, Pine Brook Inn north of Stroudsburg to the Rev. Percy Crawford, the Fulmer House [*now the Best Western Pocono Inn*], the old Fair Grounds on West Main Street (now Stroud Union High School), the former J.J. Newberry Store property on Main Street, and the Main Street property on which the Sherman Theater is now located.

I never regretted the decision to make real estate my career.  For over thirty years I was privileged to participate directly in the growth and development of Monroe County and the Delaware Valley   the area where I have resided all my life and for which I have an abiding affection.

**See BUSHKILL FALLS**

*Niagara of Pennsylvania*

ROUTE 209

**Frank LeBar** REAL ESTATE *and* SECURITIES
601 Thomas St. Stroudsburg, Pa.

From *Secrets of Pocono Kitchens*, compiled by Women's Auxiliary, Stroudsburg Presbyterian Church, 1942

# INDEX

People, places and subjects mentioned in the text. Page numbers of illustrations are in italic. All places are in Pennsylvania, unless otherwise noted.